United Year

The full story of Manchester United's '94-'95 Season

Compiled by
DAVID EMERY

SIMON & SCHUSTER

LONDON • SYDNEY • NEW YORK • TOKYO • TORONTO

First published in Great Britain by Simon & Schuster Ltd, 1995
A Viacom Company

Simon & Schuster Ltd
West Garden Place
Kendal Street
London W2 2AQ

Simon & Schuster of Australia Pty Ltd
Sydney

A CIP catalogue record for this book is available from the British
Library.

ISBN 0-671-51180-7

Typeset by The Imaging Business

**Printed and bound in Great Britain by
Butler & Tanner Ltd, Frome and London**

Contents

For news, reports and independent information on
Manchester United in the 1995/1996 season call
0891-137-218

For all the news throughout the 1995/96 soccer season
call the Daily Express Soccer line 0891-204-270
calls cost 39p per minute cheap rate
and 49p per minute at all other times

Prices correct at time of going to press

In Brief

By John Bean

Alex Ferguson will have pondered long and hard about the championship that got away in the last match of a campaign of draconian drama.

Manchester United, the artists, were beaten by a point by Blackburn the artisans. But what would have happened if Eric Cantona hadn't been ripped out of the final third of the season?

In reality United, reinforced by the arrival of Andy Cole and the legs and lungs of their superb youngsters, coped well enough with the absence of the most gifted player in Britain. Ten wins and four draws from the 16 league games that followed the Frenchman's brainstorm at Selhurst Park on January 25, was title form. But crucially three of those draws were goalless affairs at home.

Would Cantona have unlocked the defences of Spurs, Leeds or Chelsea at Old Trafford? Did the impulsive, absent Frenchman cost Old Trafford a third successive title?

Though they touched occasional peaks, United were clearly not quite the coruscating force of the previous two championship seasons without Cantona.

There was also another limited run in Europe. But the quality of their kindergarden, the immediate impact of new £7-million striker Andy Cole and another Wembley run was some consolation.

In 17 games, plus one as substitute, after his £7-million January arrival at Old Trafford, Cole got a dozen goals.

In the Cup Final United's 58-match season at home and abroad ended in defeat by Everton. So the famous old pot was torn from their grasp at the wire. It was that sort of campaign. But what a season it was...

We'll be back . . .

The Matches

MANCHESTER UNITED 2

QPR 0

(Half-time-time score : 0-0)

United: Schmeichel, May (Parker 70), Irwin, Bruce, Sharpe (Keane 70), Pallister, Kanchelskis, Ince, McClair, Hughes, Giggs.
Sub: Pilkington.
QPR: Roberts, Bardsley, Wilson, Yates, Gallen (Maddix 88), McDonald, Impey, Holloway, Ferdinand (Penrice 82), Barker, Sinclair.
Scorers: Hughes 47, McClair 68.
Referee: D Gallagher (Banbury).
Attendance: 43,214

You could not get two full-backs further removed from the bear-trap tacklers who leave scar tissue on the opposition than Paul Parker and Clive Wilson. But, as United shifted into gear for the new season, both defenders learned that the FA's clean-up campaign would mop up the good guys as well as the bad.

Under the new rules both had to be sent off, Wilson after eight minutes with the grass of Old Trafford scarcely trampled when his angled tackle near the touchline felled the flying Andrei Kanchelskis.

Last season referee Dermot Gallagher might have been able to use his discretion. Certainly the dismissal left the 43,214 fans wondering if tackling was to be consigned to football's museum along with the leather ball and metal-tipped boots.

"I didn't expect to be the first guy in the rogues' gallery," said Wilson.

The problem, as Rangers manager Gerry Francis pointed out, is that with flyers like Ryan Giggs and Kanchelskis about a touch is going to produce a yellow or red card.

Parker, a late substitute for United, went four minutes after getting on the field for taking out Les Ferdinand two yards in front of the penalty box. He got tangled up. But again, under the new rules, he had to go.

Even Ferdinand sympathised: "We're talking about two of the cleanest defenders in the game here. Both made genuine attempts to win the ball. It's a shame. Unless we get this sorted out we'll be talking about sendings off for months to come."

With a plethora of attacking talent on his books, United manager Alex Ferguson knows his club will benefit more than most from the crackdown. Mark Hughes should be the biggest beneficiary. The Welshman rarely gets through a game without defenders targeting the back of his ankles.

It made a pleasant change for Hughes who looked in fine shape as he turned on to a Kanchelskis pass after 47 minutes to fire home the first. "You always get a few tackles from behind," he said. "But today the defenders didn't get their usual quota."

This was not the explosive, creative United of much of last season.

No doubt the suspended Eric Cantona, sitting on the bench under a baseball hat, would have made a difference.

Instead it was left to Paul Ince's huge efforts in midfield, echoing the £8,000-a-week deal he had signed the previous night, to provide the inspiration. It was Ince's shot against the bar in the 68th minute that sealed it for United because Brian McClair nodded in the rebound.

Rangers had the consolation of introducing an 18-year-old attacker, Kevin Gallen, who looked special. You don't cock a snook at defenders like Gary Pallister, especially at Old Trafford. But Gallen did. He could have scored, too, if he had not controlled one break with his hand and fired across a gaping net in another.

The most disconsolate figure at the end was Wilson. "I thought you had to be the last defender and pulling the other bloke down before you got sent off," he complained. "What a start to the season!"

Clive Wilson brings down Andrei Kanchelskis and is sent off.

League Table After Match

	P	W	D	L	F	A	Pts
Liverpool	1	1	0	0	6	1	3
Arsenal	1	1	0	0	3	0	3
Newcastle	1	1	0	0	3	1	3
Chelsea	1	1	0	0	2	0	3
Man Utd	1	1	0	0	2	0	3
Tottenham	1	1	0	0	4	3	3
Nottm Forest	1	1	0	0	1	0	3
Aston Villa	1	0	1	0	2	2	1
Everton	1	0	1	0	2	2	1
Blackburn	1	0	1	0	1	1	1
Coventry	1	0	1	0	1	1	1
Southampton	1	0	1	0	1	1	1
Wimbledon	1	0	1	0	1	1	1
Leeds	1	0	1	0	0	0	1
West Ham	1	0	1	0	0	0	1
Sheff Wed	1	0	0	1	3	4	0
Ipswich	1	0	0	1	0	1	0
Leicester	1	0	0	1	1	3	0
Norwich	1	0	0	1	0	2	0
QPR	1	0	0	1	0	2	0
Man City	1	0	0	1	0	3	0
C Palace	1	0	0	1	1	6	0

August 22

NOTTINGHAM FOREST 1

MANCHESTER UNITED 1

(Half-time score : 1-1)

Forest: Crossley, Lyttle, Pearce, Cooper, Chettle, Phillips, Gemmill, Collymore, Stone, Woan, Roy (Bohinen 80).
United: Schmeichel, May, Irwin, Bruce, Sharpe, Pallister, Ince, McClair, Hughes, Giggs (Keane 56), Kanchelskis.
Subs: Parker, Pilkington.
Scorer: (Forest): Collymore 26; (United): Kanchelskis 22.
Referee: A Wilkie (Chester-le-Street).
Attendance: 22,072

Manchester United had their pedigree tested by the new striking partnership that threatens to terrorise the Premiership. Bryan Roy and Stan Collymore have come together from opposite ends of football's spectrum but at Forest's City Ground they played like blood brothers.

It was Collymore – who has arrived via Stafford, Crystal Palace reserves and Southend - who replied to Andrei Kanchelskis' inspired 22nd-minute goal with a superb equaliser.

Collymore's partner Roy, of course, arrived via Italy and the World Cup Finals. But their chemistry has been instant and explosive.

United boss Alex Ferguson, who takes his Old Trafford aristocrats to Tottenham in the next match, admitted: "I saw Jurgen Klinsmann play at Hillsborough on TV. He's a great player but he won't cause us any more problems than young Collymore tonight. He takes on players, is big and powerful and is always looking to shoot with either foot."

United, of course, will treat this as nothing more than the mildest hiccup at this stage of the season, though the game did underline one worrying fact for Ferguson. It is that without the imperious Eric Cantona, who still has one more match of his three-game ban to serve, United looked like a thoroughbred without a jockey.

We have come to expect football of radar-like understanding from the champions. That it also came from Forest was something of a surprise, particularly as it was accompanied by a gutsy defiance and a will to slug it out.

Games of this heady quality are being produced partly because of the new directive on the laws, which protect the good player, and referee Alan Wilkie applied them with common sense. It led to bookings for Des Lyttle, Bryan Roy, Ian Woan and Forest old boy Roy Keane.

United owed much to Peter Schmeichel, their defiant Dane, who made courageous saves from Collymore and Roy. Mark Crossley was not exactly slothful in the Forest goal and his early save from a savage Denis Irwin free kick was crucial. Then Collymore, drifting from his central role to unsettle United's central defenders, emerged as the game's dominant figure with his willingness to pepper the target.

United's goal when it came was one to match that scored by Ince in the Charity Shield. Lee Sharpe hit a dipping cross-field ball from the left and, as it fell, so Kanchelskis struck it on the volley to send the ball whistling past the amazed Crossley.

United were allowed to admire it for less than five minutes before Forest were level. It was a goal almost as spectacular, with Roy providing the neatest of back-headers to Collymore's feet. The striker turned on it in an instant and, with minimal backlift, drilled his shot inside the post.

Ryan Giggs, who had been anonymous and appearing to miss Cantona more than most, was replaced by Keane, a move which produced cries of Judas at their former player from the 22,072 crowd.

Hughes looked as if he had snatched the winner with a typically opportunist shot when Keane dummied a David May centre but Crossley somehow managed to fall on the ball.

Ince, whose combative spirit had kept United fully involved in the game, struck the upright when Sharpe laid the ball back in the 63rd minute but a winner then would have flattered United. Irwin needed to clear off the line from the excellent Colin Cooper's header five minutes later to prevent defeat against a Forest team whose return to the Premiership will clearly be an attractive addition.

Andrei Kanchelskis lets fly a fabulously angled volley to seal a point for his team.

League Table After Match

	P	W	D	L	F	A	Pts
Newcastle	2	2	0	0	7	1	6
Tottenham	2	2	0	0	6	4	6
Blackburn	2	1	1	0	4	1	4
Man Utd	2	1	1	0	3	1	4
Nottm Forest	2	1	1	0	2	1	4
Leeds	2	1	1	0	1	0	4
Liverpool	1	1	0	0	6	1	3
Arsenal	2	1	0	1	3	1	3
Chelsea	1	1	0	0	2	0	3
Man City	2	1	0	1	3	3	3
QPR	2	1	0	1	3	4	3
Aston Villa	2	0	2	0	3	3	2
Southampton	2	0	2	0	2	2	2
Wimbledon	2	0	2	0	2	2	2
Everton	2	0	1	1	3	4	1
Ipswich	2	0	1	1	1	2	1
Norwich	2	0	1	1	0	2	1
West Ham	2	0	1	1	0	3	1
Coventry	2	0	1	1	1	5	1
C Palace	2	0	1	1	1	6	1
Sheff Wed	2	0	0	2	4	7	0
Leicester	2	0	0	2	1	6	0

August 27

TOTTENHAM HOTSPUR 0
MANCHESTER UNITED 1
(Half-time score : 0-0)

Tottenham: Walker, Edinburgh, Calderwood (Hazard 57), Barmby, Dumitrescu, Anderton, Sheringham, Nethercott, Klinsmann, Kerslake, Campbell.
United: Schmeichel, Irwin, Bruce, Sharpe, Pallister, Ince, McClair, Hughes, Giggs, May, Kanchelskis.
Subs: Dublin, Pilkington.
Scorer: Bruce 49.
Referee: K W Burge (Mid Glamorgan).
Attendance: 24,502

Peter Schmeichel has occasionally been a snappy, yappy watchdog in the United goal, but when Tottenham showed him their new teeth at White Hart Lane, he was a Great Dane again.

It was a crucial transformation for this was a match decided by goal-keeping merit. In the new climate of the game, where the man in possession of the ball is favoured, a sharper focus has been thrown on those who form the last line of defence.

Poor Ian Walker, deputising for Erik Thorstvedt, stumbled over the heel of his full-back Justin Edinburgh and was helpless as Steve Bruce headed into the empty goal where the goalkeeper should have been standing four minutes after half-time.

At the other end Schmeichel flung himself to his right to hold a Teddy Sheringham penalty and then made outstanding saves from Jurgen Klinsmann and Nicky Barmby. United manager Alex Ferguson suggested later that this might be the only time this season that a team faces Tottenham and comes away with a clean sheet.

"Because of the way they play under Ossie Ardiles and the type of players they have, they are going to create chances," said Ferguson. "They made half a dozen in the last 20 minutes which could have given us a bad result."

Not with Schmeichel about. Even the most prolific of forwards have faced the Dane and seen a goal that looks as small as the hole on the last green when you need a five-foot putt to the win the golf match.

Klinsmann may well have recalled what Schmeichel did for Denmark in the final of the European Championships when the German also drew a blank against him.

Bruce said: "He is a fantastic goalkeeper. He has been making those kind of saves for the last two years now and has proved himself the top goalkeeper in Europe."

Tottenham could take heart from the fact that they will play a lot worse than this and win. Meanwhile, United are poised two points behind Kevin Keegan's pace-setting Newcastle with the three-match ban on Eric Cantona duly served.

When the Frenchman is missing United are like a cluster of emeralds without the central diamond, still able to sparkle but not with an intensity that makes you take a sharp breath.

Ryan Giggs, yet to come good this season, is one who cannot wait for his return. Even so, this was an important victory for United who want to stay in touch with the top of the table before the European Cup diversion begins against Gothenburg at Old Trafford.

Meanwhile Sheringham will muse about his second penalty failure in four days and ask himself whether he would be better passing the responsibility to Ilie Dumitrescu – outstanding in the second half – or Klinsmann.

Spurs boss Ardiles said: "I am disappointed we lost but happy with the performance. "How many teams have felt they played well against United, yet come away with nothing?

The first published Premiership table shows Newcastle, Blackburn and United occupying the top slots. It would be a rash punter who bets against one of them lifting the ultimate prize next spring.

League Table After Match

	P	W	D	L	F	A	Pts
Newcastle	3	3	0	0	12	2	9
Blackburn	3	2	1	0	8	1	7
Man Utd	3	2	1	0	4	1	7
Nottm Forest	3	2	1	0	3	1	7
Liverpool	2	2	0	0	9	1	6
Man City	3	2	0	1	7	3	6
Chelsea	2	2	0	0	5	2	6
Tottenham	3	2	0	1	6	5	6
Ipswich	3	1	1	1	3	3	4
Leeds	3	1	1	1	3	3	4
Norwich	3	1	1	1	1	2	4
Aston Villa	3	0	3	0	4	4	3
Sheff Wed	3	1	0	2	6	7	3
Arsenal	3	1	0	2	3	4	3
QPR	3	1	0	2	4	6	3
Wimbledon	3	0	2	1	2	3	2
Southampton	3	0	2	1	3	7	2
C Palace	3	0	2	1	2	7	2
West Ham	3	0	1	2	0	4	1
Everton	3	0	1	2	3	8	1
Coventry	3	0	1	2	1	9	1
Leicester	3	0	0	3	1	7	0

Ilie Dumitrescu tackles the England star Paul Ince.

August 31

MANCHESTER UNITED 3
WIMBLEDON 0
(Half-time score : 1-0)

United: Schmeichel, May, Irwin, Bruce, Sharpe, Pallister, Kanchelskis, Cantona, McClair, Hughes, Giggs.
Subs: Butt, Dublin, Pilkington.
Wimbledon: Segers, Barton, Elkins, Jones, Talboys, Fitzgerald, Ardley, Castledine (Clarke 65), Harford, Kimble, Gayle.
Scorers: Cantona 40, McClair 81, Giggs 84.
Referee: T J Holbrook (Walsall).
Attendance: 43,440

Eric Cantona returned to centre stage at Old Trafford with a goal that blazed his genius across the famous stadium.

United boss Alex Ferguson admitted the magic had been missing from his side's start to the season, with the French maestro banned from the first three games. Cantona, who had squinted under his baseball cap from the United bench during that time, quickly reminded us of his special quality. And his headed goal five minutes before the interval was a signal to the rest of the Premiership that last season's PFA Player of the Year was back on centre stage as good as ever.

Ferguson said: "Eric at his brilliant best is a calming influence for us. He gives us an extra dimension and has an aura that all great players possess."

Joe Kinnear's Wimbledon usually enjoy playing the role of Little Big Men at Old Trafford. Two seasons earlier Vinnie Jones almost peeled the paint from the dressing-room wall as he paraded with his ghetto blaster celebrating a famous league win. But with five of his players sitting it out here – Dean Holdsworth, Gary Blissett, Robbie Earle, John Scales and Dean Blackwell – even the ebullient Kinnear could not have expected a repeat.

It still needed a touch of quality to beat the Wimbledon defence and it was supplied by Ryan Giggs and Cantona. The Welsh winger beat two defenders and flung over a perfectly measured cross for the Frenchman to crash home a bullet header in the 40th minute.

With Brian McClair and Giggs adding further goals in the last nine minutes it was compelling evidence that United have no intention of letting their eyes be diverted by the dazzle of another European Cup tilt.

A Jones blunder 35 yards out let in McClair, who hammered a powerful shot into the roof of the net. Three minutes later Giggs played a one-two with Mark Hughes and knocked in the third.

But the most chilling sight for United's Premiership rivals was Cantona's lean, mean look as he set about making up for lost time. The Dons hardly laid a boot on him as he dropped deep to avoid direct contact with their defenders. Even poor Jones, subject of torment and ridicule from the 43,440 crowd, could do nothing as the

French ace shredded the defence with pin-point passes.

Paul Ince was missing from the United midfield with tendinitis, leaving Lee Sharpe to patrol alongside McClair.

Mick Harford tried manfully to plug the gap left up front by the £1.25 million sale of John Fashanu to Aston Villa but it was always going to be a tough night for Wimbledon. "We had so many players missing," lamented Kinnear. "It was certainly the wrong time to meet a side of United's quality."

McClair runs back after scoring for United.

September 11

LEEDS 2
MANCHESTER UNITED 1
(Half-time score : 1-0)

Leeds: Lukic, Kelly, Palmer, Wetherall, Worthington, White (Deane 31), McAllister, Speed, Wallace, Masinga (Fairclough 87), Whelan.
United: Schmeichel, May, Bruce, Pallister, Irwin, Kanchelskis, McClair (Butt 63), Ince, Giggs (Sharpe 63), Hughes, Cantona.
Sub: Pilkington.
Scorers: (Leeds): Wetherall 13, Deane 49; (United): Cantona 74 pen.
Referee: D Elleray (Harrow).
Attendance: 39,396

For 13 years Manchester United have marched across the Pennines to pluck a petal from the white rose of Leeds. Yesterday all they got for their efforts was a crown of thorns.

The celebration that followed this Leeds victory in front of a delirious crowd of 39,396 was indicative of a series of results that have plagued the Yorkshire public.

Even in this hectic meeting Leeds were left hanging on in the final 15 minutes after referee David Elleray threw Alex Ferguson's side an unexpected lifeline. Elleray, who gave United a controversial penalty against Chelsea in last season's FA Cup final, did so again and Eric Cantona again took advantage.

Leeds manager Howard Wilkinson had clearly done his homework thoroughly and decided that, if there was a weakness in the champions' armoury, it was at right-back, where David May has yet to be fully integrated. Leeds probed that flank like a dentist's drill on a sensitive tooth and both goals came from there. This raw nerve heel will doubtless have been noted by the watching Gothenburg assistant manager Ruben Svensson, as it must have been, with alarm, by Ferguson himself.

But, if the goals came from this source, it was Leeds' midfield pairing of Gary McAllister and Gary Speed who pumped the balls into it. Despite the energy and resource of Paul Ince, with lung-busting running and clawing tackles, Leeds always held the edge in midfield, enabling their forwards to trouble Steve Bruce and Gary Pallister.

Leeds owed much to Noel Whelan, a teenage striker of sinewy frame and elusive movement whose partnership with South African Phil Masinga looks full of menace.

United never achieved a rhythm, partly because of an uncharacteristically poor game from Andrei Kanchelskis and a lack of penetration from Ryan Giggs. Cantona tried to lift the forward line with his repertoire of flicks and feints but his colleagues consistently failed to respond.

So it was from enterprising Leeds that the main threat came, and their opening goal in the 13th minute was fully deserved, albeit a trifle fortunate. David White's driven corner was missed by Speed and hit

Bruce. As the ball bounced out, David Weatherall mis-hit his shot and the ball bobbled over the line.

Giggs ought to have cancelled that out when Cantona put him through with a delicate chip, but John Lukic had read it well and came out to save.

It was a full-blooded contest and Elleray, a Harrow schoolmaster, was forced to administer the cane. May was the first of seven bookings, the other six were all being Leeds players. Cantona escaped punishment, though his two-footed challenge on McAllister was perhaps the most sinister tackle of the afternoon.

The Frenchman, however, almost scored the goal of the season, juggling Pallister's pass from one foot to the other in front of a bemused Carlton Palmer before shooting just past the far post.

Brian Deane replaced the injured White after half an hour and should have scored on half-time but he ballooned the ball over from inside the six-yard area. He atoned for that after 48 minutes when Whelan again probed the United right flank, swaying past May and Pallister and squaring the ball for Deane to drive home.

The introduction of Nicky Butt and Lee Sharpe after 62 minutes changed the flow, and concerted United pressure brought a heavy challenge from Deane on Ince a good yard outside the penalty area. Mr Elleray, though, decided it was a penalty and Cantona does not miss. It gave Leeds an anxious last 15 minutes, Hughes volleying over and Bruce squandering a header in injury time.

It was 12 months to the date that United lost to Chelsea on the Saturday before their opening game in the European Cup. Then Ferguson had shuffled his line-up to try out his European formation. This time he could field his strongest available side.

But Leeds deserved this act of revenge for the courage with which they took on their illustrious opponents with a five-man attack. They defended stoically, too, and were orchestrated imaginatively in midfield. For once it was the red rose that looked in need of a little careful gardening.

League Table After Match

	P	W	D	L	F	A	Pts
Newcastle	5	5	0	0	19	5	15
Nottm Forest	5	4	1	0	9	3	13
Blackburn	5	3	2	0	11	1	11
Liverpool	4	3	1	0	11	1	10
Man Utd	5	3	1	1	8	3	10
Leeds	5	3	1	1	7	5	10
Chelsea	4	3	0	1	10	6	9
Tottenham	4	3	0	1	9	6	9
Aston Villa	5	2	3	0	7	4	9
Man City	5	2	1	2	8	7	7
Norwich	5	1	3	1	1	2	6
Arsenal	5	1	2	2	3	4	5
QPR	5	1	2	2	7	9	5
Wimbledon	5	1	2	2	4	7	5
Sheff Wed	5	1	1	3	7	11	4
Ipswich	5	1	1	3	4	8	4
C Palace	5	0	3	2	4	10	3
Southampton	4	0	2	2	3	9	2
West Ham	5	0	2	3	1	7	2
Coventry	5	0	2	3	3	12	2
Leicester	5	0	1	4	3	10	1
Everton	5	0	1	4	4	13	1

September 14

MANCHESTER UNITED 4
IFK GOTHENBURG 2
(Half-time score : 1-1)

United: Schmeichel, May, Irwin, Bruce, Sharpe, Pallister, Kanchelskis, Ince, Butt, Hughes, Giggs.
IFK: Ravelli, Kamark, Johansson, Bjorklund, Nilsson, Martinsson, Erlingmark, Lindqvist, Blomqvist, Olsson (Rehn 44), Pettersson.
Scorers: (IFK): Pettersson 26, Rehn 50; (United): Giggs 33, 65, Kanchelskis 48, Sharpe 70.
Referee: Goethals (Belgium).
Attendance: 33,625

Alex Ferguson hailed a masterly performance from Paul Ince after the England midfielder put his injury worries behind him to power United to an opening Champions' League win at Old Trafford. "He was magnificent," said the United manager. "I spoke beforehand about the challenge ahead for our players and Paul responded to every test put before him."

Ince, the player hailed at Old Trafford as the new Bryan Robson, had needed an injection to ease a nagging knee injury. And after a barnstorming display in a United side seriously weakened by the absence of star personnel like Eric Cantona and Roy Keane, Ince spoke about his determination to rise to the big occasion.

"I didn't feel 100 per cent fit but had to go for it and suffer the consequences," he said. "I feel sore now but I'll be there on the team sheet for the visit of Liverpool on Saturday."

United needed the inspiration of Ince to maintain their superb record of not having lost a European match at Old Trafford for 38 years and 54 ties. The route was hazardous as they conceded a 26th-minute goal against the 18-times Swedish champions and later surrendered the lead before Giggs and Lee Sharpe carried the two points into safe custody.

The absence of Eric Cantona through suspension was muted by the contribution of Nicky Butt, who came of age in a memorable European debut.

Alongside Ince, Giggs and Butt were other commanding performances. Sharpe added his postscript to the night with a splendid goal and Andrei Kanchelskis showed why he must not be left out of these 18-carat occasions.

In defence there were times when David May over-committed himself and occasions when United needed Peter Schmeichel to perform his bodyguard duties. He might have been at fault for the first goal but his subsequent performance atoned.

It was clear United could expect no protection from Belgian referee Guy Goethals, who appeared to have left the Fifa letter on new refereeing directives unopened in the envelope. He turned a Nelsonian eye to some of the more physical excesses.

In the opening minutes Giggs teased and tormented while the rest responded. Goalkeeper Tomas Ravelli, last seen in acrobatic action in the World Cup, was having his fingertips warmed on this chilly Manchester night, touching shots from Kanchelskis and Denis Irwin over his crossbar.

It was pot-shot time, then out of nowhere came the counter-punch. Schmeichel had barely touched the ball before he came out rather lethargically to meet Mikael Martinsson's centre. He did not touch it then either. Stefan Pettersson stuck out his right foot and scored.

That lead lasted little more than five minutes as Mark Hughes went on the rampage, driving a low cross into the six-yard box. Sharpe's shot rebounded off Pontus Kamark and Giggs was handily placed to apply the finishing strike.

United took control. Gary Pallister headed out a Giggs corner to the edge of the area and Kanchelskis drilled the ball back through the pack and into the net.

United surrendered that lead within 90 seconds as the Swedes won a free-kick 25 yards out. Mikael Nilsson's shot seemed to be covered until former Evertonian Stefan Rehn stuck out a leg and deflected it past Schmeichel.

Back came United. Ince drove onwards relentlessly. Sharpe shot from 30 yards, Ravelli could only touch the ball on to the bar and again Giggs was waiting for the scraps. And when Ravelli failed to come for a Kanchelskis cross in the 70th minute, Sharpe punished him with a flourish.

It was comprehensive enough in the end but nerve-ends had been stretched like guitar strings.

"It was a marvellous result for us but when we lost that first goal I thought it was going to be one of those nights, another piece of suicide," confessed Ferguson. "There is always a question about your team's character when they go behind like that but they recovered admirably to prove they don't lack it."

United captain Steve Bruce said: "People have been saying we would struggle in the Champions' Cup without Eric Cantona. The same people used to say United were not the same team without Bryan Robson. But we learned to live without Robbo and tonight we have shown we can survive without Eric."

September 17

MANCHESTER UNITED 2
LIVERPOOL 0
(Half-time score : 0-0)

United: Schmeichel, May, Irwin, Bruce, Kanchelskis, Pallister, Cantona, Ince, Sharpe, Hughes (McClair 59), Giggs.
Subs: Butt, Pilkington.
Liverpool: James, Jones, Bjornebye, Scales, Ruddock, Molby (Babb 70), Redknapp, McManaman, Rush, Barnes, Fowler.
Scorers: Kanchelskis 71, McClair 73.
Referee: K Morton (Bury St Edmunds).
Attendance: 43,740

They sat on their benches discussing the vital moves they had made and there was no doubt that Alex Ferguson had checkmated Roy Evans.

There had been rumblings of discontent from another huge Old Trafford crowd when Ferguson withdrew his knight Mark Hughes and shuffled his pieces, pushing his king Eric Cantona into an advanced position and employing his castle Brian McClair in a deeper role.

Evans countered by withdrawing his rounded bishop Jan Molby and putting on his own knight in Phil Babb but he knew within a couple of minutes that he had been out-manoeuvred and there was to be no escape.

There have been some fascinating games between United and Liverpool and this one lived up to expectations, the passing and movement at times reaching mesmerising levels.

Liverpool will be disappointed they got nothing from the contest because for an hour they seemed to hold the initiative as United grappled for control of a midfield being dominated by Molby, John Barnes and Jamie Redknapp.

Ferguson knew he had to change his strategy, explaining: "For 15 minutes after half-time Liverpool ran us all over the place and it was at that point I decided to take Hughes off.

"He has been playing but not training because of a groin injury and in that situation there comes a point where you are not getting the real Sparky. He usually excels in the atmosphere and competitiveness of these games. I just felt I had to get McClair on to play against Molby because he was controlling the game.

"For the last half-hour we did really well. Once we got in front our confidence came immediately and it ended up as a terrific result for us."

Evans's decision, 12 minutes after McClair's introduction, was to remove the tiring Molby and give Babb his first taste of the action in an advanced midfield role.

Liverpool's boss said: "After McClair came on we started to get overrun and I made the change to get fresh legs and hopefully relieve the pressure. In hindsight Alex made a good substitution and I made a bad one.

"That's the way this game goes. Sometimes you get a pat on the head and others you get kicked up the backside. But we stopped doing the simple things. We suddenly thought we were better than we were."

It was refreshing self-analysis from Evans, who is impressively reinstating the old values at Liverpool, where simplicity and an honest sharing of responsibility are the tested ethics.

The intensity of the rivalry between the fans may not diminish but there seems to be a genuine and friendly respect between Ferguson and Evans which was never apparent when Kenny Dalglish and Graeme Souness held the Anfield reins.

It even extended to Fergie backing Evans. "I thought he had made the right substitution for that time of the game. Substitutions are a manager's nightmare. I had decided Babb would start the game, so my pre-match team talk meant nothing!"

Evans responded: "And I picked Brian McClair to start in the position you brought him on. Maybe we should swap jobs."

It was good, open banter from two managers you suspect might have more telephone chats than we imagine between Mondays and Fridays. A talk with Cantona is what Ferguson must have this morning about the red mist that once again came over him late in the game and which might have cost him another three-match ban.

Cantona felt Neil Ruddock should have been punished for a forearm jab under his neck. When referee Kelvin Morton took no action the old eye-for-an-eye instinct for swift retribution took over and Cantona was fortunate that it was a yellow and not a red card that was shown for his two-footed lunge of revenge.

Cantona tapped his head to suggest Ruddock might be a woodentop but he is insulting his own intelligence when he risks a suspension that would be as damaging to himself as it is to the rest of the team. He should know by now there are defenders who delight in ruffling him and should rise above the temptation to sink to their level.

United opened the scoring when John Scales, who played almost faultlessly in the first half, was guilty of a sloppy headed backpass

League Table After Match

	P	W	D	L	F	A	Pts
Newcastle	6	6	0	0	22	7	18
Blackburn	6	4	2	0	13	2	14
Nottm Forest	6	4	2	0	10	4	14
Man Utd	6	4	1	1	10	3	13
Liverpool	5	3	1	1	11	3	10
Leeds	6	3	1	2	8	7	10
Chelsea	5	3	0	2	11	8	9
Aston Villa	6	2	3	1	7	5	9
Tottenham	6	3	0	3	11	11	9
Norwich	6	2	3	1	3	3	9
Man City	6	2	2	2	9	8	8
QPR	6	1	3	2	9	11	6
Wimbledon	6	1	3	2	4	7	6
Southampton	6	1	3	2	6	11	6
Arsenal	6	1	2	3	5	7	5
Sheff Wed	6	1	2	3	8	12	7
West Ham	6	1	2	3	2	7	5
Coventry	6	1	2	3	5	13	5
Leicester	6	1	1	4	6	11	4
Ipswich	6	1	1	4	5	10	4
C Palace	6	0	4	2	4	10	4
Everton	6	0	2	4	6	15	2

and Andrei Kanchelskis pounced. Kanchelskis was involved in the second, too, playing the ball on and watching as McClair and Cantona exchanged passes exquisitely in the box for the Scot to slide home his third goal of the season.

A week that started badly at Leeds had turned into a highly satisfactory one with two European and three Premier League points. "You always want to win the big ones," said Fergie. "We didn't at Leeds and maybe that was the kick up the backside we needed."

Evans responded: "We have had a kick in the teeth today but we now have to be self-motivated. We have to use this result in the same way Alex used the Leeds result. You don't lay down and die."

It is back to the chess board for Evans, but the way he is going about his job Liverpool are not destined to be the pawns in the Premier League.

Kanchelskis acrobatically slots the ball in, watched by Neil Ruddock.

September 21

Alex Ferguson sent out a reserve side for the Coca-Cola competition he regards as a major irritant. But he had the satisfaction of discovering that, even with six kids in the team at Vale Park, United had the beating of John Rudge's First Division outfit.

Fergie can point to the goals young Paul Scholes picked out with the precision of a locksmith as evidence of the prodigious talent on the fringes of his 25m dressing-room.

With four competitions in his diary, Ferguson did not want to be involved in this particular piece of silverware. His obvious disdain for it provoked condemnation from local Labour MPs. Joan Walley, Labour MP for Stoke-on-Trent North, said: "The fans wanted to see Giggs and Cantona. They wanted to see United's stars. There should be a full inquiry".

Nine players were missing from the side which had beaten Liverpool the previous Saturday. But an unrepentant Ferguson insisted: "I will be doing this throughout the Coca-Cola Cup. With a big European match next week and internationals and other other events looming, most people expect us to do the sensible thing. We are doing what is right for United. The inexperience of my side helped them tonight. They did not have a care and played with no fear."

If a United Pontins League outfit containing five 19-year-olds can beat Vale, one wonders what their full assembly of stars would have done. Vale, having scored inside the first 10 minutes, never justified their seventh place in the First Division.

Bradley Sandeman struck a magnificent 20-yard half-volley that was deflected past United's stand-in keeper Gary Walsh by Lee Glover's head. But United's kids settled, gained control and hit back through Scholes' fine chipped shot nine minutes before the break.

With United's shadow squad clamping on their authority in the second half, Scholes headed home the winner.

PORT VALE 1
MANCHESTER UNITED 2
(Half-time score : 1-1)

Port Vale: Musselwhite, Sandeman, Tankard, Porter, Griffiths, D. Glover, Kent, Van der Laan, Foyle, L. Glover, Naylor (Burke 71).
United: Walsh, Neville (O'Kane 76), Irwin, Butt (Sharpe 82), May, Keane, Gillespie, Beckham, McClair, Scholes, Davies.
Sub: Pilkington.
Scorers: (Port Vale): L. Glover 7; (United): Scholes 36, 53.
Referee: J Lloyd (Wrexham).
Attendance: 18,605

September 24

IPSWICH 3
MANCHESTER UNITED 2
(Half-time score : 2-0)

Ipswich: Forest, Yallop, Wark (Milton 88), Linighan, Johnson, Mason, Williams, Palmer, Sedgley, Thomsen, Paz (Guentchev 77).
United: Walsh, Keane, Bruce, Pallister, Irwin, Sharpe (Scholes 62), Ince, Kanchelskis, Cantona, McClair, Giggs.
Subs: Butt, Pilkington.
Scorers: (Ipswich): Mason 15, 43, Sedgley 80; (United): Cantona 71, Scholes 73.
Referee: P Jones (Loughborough).
Attendance: 22,559

Maybe it was a half-time tongue lashing from Alex Ferguson or his decision to switch the disappointing Roy Keane from midfield to right back. Whatever it was, United were a more potent team in the second 45 minutes even if they were too late to save themselves from a shock defeat from the Premiership's strugglers.

As well as a new position, Keane may need to discover a new temperament to guarantee a successful future at Manchester United. The Irish international should have been sent off for a despicably high, studs-up lunge at Steve Palmer in the first half after losing his head for 20 minutes. Ferguson refused to talk about Keane but his decision to switch the Irishman to right-back from central midfield for the second half spoke volumes.

But at right-back Keane was a revelation, inspiring a comeback with some surging runs down the flank. He provided two low drilled crosses in two minutes for Cantona and teenage substitute Paul Scholes to make it 2-2 after Ipswich had gone 2-0 up in the first half through goals by Paul Mason.

United dominated this vibrant game by any footballing criterion skill, technique, possession, shots on target and corners won. But Ipswich more than matched them for passion and courage.

Ten minutes from time Steve Sedgley earned the East Anglians their first home victory since February with a shot which deflected into the net off Keane. The other moment which summed up the match was Ipswich's first goal. Paul Ince hit the bar with a crashing header in the 15th minute and sat dumbstruck in the penalty area for something like 30 seconds. By the time he got up Ipswich had broken away through a vacant midfield to score.

Ferguson's view on Ince's uncharacteristic folly would surely have been unprintable, certainly according to Ipswich coach Paul Goddard.

"Our passion was fantastic today and it was a great way to end the week after two defeats. But no one should write off United for anything. They're still an outstanding team; just as good as last year. You only have to sit in the dug-out and hear what they get from the bench. Screaming and shouting goes on every time a player makes even one mistake."

Maybe it is fire and rage which forges champions. Or maybe it is another indication that United have not discovered how to lose with good grace. Their silent exit from Portman Road in a depressing downpour did them no credit.

Paul Mason cuts through the defence to put Ipswich up on the champions.

League Table After Match

	P	W	D	L	F	A	Pts
Newcastle	7	6	1	0	23	8	19
Blackburn	7	5	2	0	16	3	17
Nottm Forest	7	5	2	0	14	5	17
Man Utd	7	4	1	2	12	6	13
Chelsea	6	4	0	2	12	8	12
Liverpool	6	3	2	1	12	4	11
Man City	7	3	2	2	11	8	11
Leeds	6	3	1	2	8	7	10
Aston Villa	7	2	3	2	8	8	9
Wimbledon	7	2	3	2	5	7	9
Norwich	7	2	3	2	3	5	9
Tottenham	7	3	0	4	12	15	9
Southampton	7	2	3	2	9	12	9
Arsenal	7	2	2	3	7	7	8
Ipswich	7	2	1	4	8	12	7
QPR	7	1	3	3	9	12	6
Sheff Wed	6	1	2	3	8	12	5
Leicester	7	1	2	4	7	12	5
West Ham	7	1	2	4	2	9	5
Coventry	7	1	2	4	6	16	5
C Palace	7	0	4	3	4	11	4
Everton	7	0	3	4	7	16	3

September 28

GALATASARAY 0

MANCHESTER UNITED 0

(Half-time score : 0-0)

Galatasaray: Stauche, Bulent, Sedat, Mert, Mapeza, Tugay (Arif 45), Yusuf, Kubilay, Hamza, Saffet, Hakan.
United: Schmeichel, May, Bruce, Pallister, Sharpe, Keane, Ince, Kanchelskis, Butt, Hughes, Giggs (Parker 65).
Referee: M van der Ende (Netherlands).
Attendance: 30,000

Alex Ferguson's champions showed they have the moral fibre to complement their fancy football as they went back to the scene of last season's European Cup disappointment.

This may not have been the classic United, full of flowing movement and heady rhythm, but the austere side of their character demonstrated here will be just as essential if the dream of winning the European Cup is to be fulfilled.

United were like a turbo-charged sports car cruising in the middle lane, refusing to go flat out for fear of a collision. Ferguson will be happy to have got past this obstacle with a point, one that was earned with great determination and concentration.

The United manager had set a target of eight points for qualification from the Champions' League and, with Barcelona losing to Gothenburg, United top their section by a point after two games.

This was a night of highs and lows for the English champions. Several players built on established reputations while others came away in need of self-examination. In defence United were outstanding. Peter Schmeichel may have his moments of madness but last night, as they looked up at him, the Turkish forwards must have felt they were viewing the face of Everest.

In front of Schmeichel the United defence kept their shape against some sharp counter-attacking, with Gary Pallister standing at its heart like an unbending oak. They were supported stoically by Ince, working with the energy of a man being paid piece-work wages.

Ferguson's decision to make Irishman Denis Irwin the foreign player to stand down paved the way for young Nicky Butt to stiffen the midfield, a tall order for a man of so little campaign experience.

It was a huge test in an intimidating arena. The Ali Sami Ten Stadium is not a place for anyone of nervous disposition. The youngster's early faltering steps bore testimony to that but he emerged from the 90 minutes with his stature enhanced.

The same was true of Roy Keane, whose contribution was tireless and unselfish. If United were let down it was by Ryan Giggs, whose short hair-cut seems to have had a Samson effect. Increasingly he is a man rich on promise but short on fulfilment.

Giggs' anticipated supply into the box from the left became a trickle, leaving Andrei Kanchelskis as the principal source for Mark Hughes. Hughes ploughed a lone furrow up front and almost achieved the improbable in the second half with an overhead kick that hit keeper Gintares Stauche.

There was concern for United when Ince fell clutching his arm in the second minute after a challenge with Zimbabwean Norman Mapeza but after treatment he was able to continue.

Butt was casual with a pass to Ince after 17 minutes and Tugay intercepted to set up Saffet. The striker was through on goal but hesitated, allowing Pallister to make a momentous tackle.

The tackle from behind that Kanchelskis made on Swiss international Kubilay six minutes later was less prudent and earned the Ukrainian a booking. He was followed into the book by David May. Keane let himself down by spitting at Kubilay after a late tackle and was lucky not to be spotted by the linesman.

Hughes' frustration at his lack of chances from a Cantona-less United boiled over in the 55th minute and he was cautioned for a foul on Sedat.

"This was a much better performance than last year," said Ferguson. "It is a really good result and I thought the team was very composed. We struggled a little in the first 20 minutes of the second half but recovered well to claim the point.

"It is vital we do not get carried away. In Europe, if you lose your concentration and discipline for a moment, the roof can fall in on you."

Roy Keane is sent flying by a dubious challenge from a young Turk.

October 1

MANCHESTER UNITED 2

EVERTON 0

(Half-time score : 1-0)

United: Schmeichel, May, Irwin, Bruce, Sharpe, Pallister, Cantona, Ince, Keane, Hughes (McClair 75), Kanchelskis.
Subs: Scholes, Walsh.
Everton: Southall, Rowett, Hinchcliffe, Snodin, Watson, Burrows, Samways, Stuart (Barlow 85), Unsworth, Parkinson, Amokachi.
Scorers: Kanchelskis 41, Sharpe 88.
Referee: G Poll (Tilehurst).
Attendance: 43,803

United, back from their containing operation in Istanbul, would have had to be satisfied with a draw but for the brilliance of Peter Schmeichel. The Danish goalkeeper's grasp of two thundering free-kicks from Andy Hinchcliffe and Graham Stuart gave United a most welcome three points and allowed Lee Sharpe the platform on which to demonstrate he could be just as good a match-winner as Ryan Giggs.

.Sharpe, the kid who was eclipsed at Old Trafford by the shadow of a boy two-and-a-half years his junior, makes no bones about this issue. He hates playing left-back. He quite enjoys playing left mid-field. But the role he covets most is left-wing and he is determined to fight Giggs all the way for the job.

.Sharpe's pass that cleaved Everton for the opener five minutes before the break showed why he might eventually succeed. Giggs, absent through injury, has a more versatile and original left foot. But, if you want a winger who can get to the line and hit a laser cross, Sharpe is your man.

With John Barnes' England days on the wane Sharpe believes it is the outside-left role that gives him the best chance to get into Terry Venables' dressing room.

Certainly Everton's match-plan five across midfield leaving Daniel Amokachi up front – was punctured by Sharpe. He slung across the sort of centres goalscorers feed on and this time it was Andrei Kanchelskis whose forehead made emphatic contact at the far post.

.And after Schmeichel's sure handling had kept the opposition out it was Sharpe who scuffed the clincher.

"I've told the manager how I feel," said Sharpe. "He says he doesn't see me as a left-back but needs me to play there occasionally. I see it as a straight fight between me and Giggsy on the left wing and I'm ready if the gaffer thinks his form dips. I've certainly not given up that little scrap."

While Sharpe found again the joy of flying along the wing, Everton's Amokachi was asked to run into a traffic jam up-front.

"I had four defenders against me and went past them a few times. But they won the battle because I didn't get a goal," he said. "I was the only attacker at my last club in Belgium but I'd appreciate support.

"Ideally I like to play just behind the strikers like I did for Nigeria in the World Cup. But I don't mind doing the hard job. That's what I am paid for. The pace of English football is incredible. You have to be 120 per cent fit and I need to lose three kilos."

Amokachi left with the double disappointment of a booking encouraged by Schmeichel's screaming response to the Nigerian's tackle just outside the box. Referee Graham Poll seemed intent on booking everything that moved and he was not going to miss that one.

The only puzzling aspect of United's win was Eric Cantona's muted performance. Clearly the Frenchman is suffering from a lack of match practice through his spate of bans. With a call-up due from his country, he must now miss three of United's next four outings. Clearly rust clings even to genius.

League Table After Match

	P	W	D	L	F	A	Pts
Newcastle	8	7	1	0	25	8	22
Nottm Forest	8	6	2	0	17	7	20
Blackburn	8	5	2	1	17	5	17
Man Utd	8	5	1	2	14	6	16
Liverpool	7	4	2	1	16	5	14
Leeds	8	4	2	2	11	8	14
Chelsea	7	4	0	3	13	10	12
Southampton	8	3	3	2	12	13	12
Norwich	8	3	3	2	5	6	12
Tottenham	8	4	0	4	14	16	12
Man City	8	3	2	3	11	10	11
Aston Villa	8	2	3	3	8	10	9
Wimbledon	8	2	3	3	6	9	9
Arsenal	8	2	2	4	8	9	8
West Ham	8	2	2	4	4	10	8
Ipswich	8	2	1	5	9	15	7
C Palace	8	1	4	3	6	12	7
QPR	8	1	3	4	11	15	6
Sheff Wed	8	1	3	4	10	17	6
Leicester	7	1	2	4	7	12	5
Coventry	7	1	2	4	6	16	5
Everton	8	0	3	5	7	18	3

Kanchelskis (left) scores from close range as Cantona waits.

October 5

MANCHESTER UNITED 2

PORT VALE 0

(Half-time score : 1-0)

United: Walsh, Casper, O'Kane, Butt, May, Pallister, Gillespie (Tomlinson 65), Beckham, McClair, Scholes, Davies (Neville 76).
Sub: Pilkington.
Port Vale: Musselwhite, Sandeman, Tankard, Porter, Aspin, D. Glover, Kent (Van der Laan 73), Foyle, L. Glover, Burke (Allon 73), Kelly.
Scorers: McClair 34, May 61. Agg (4-1).
Referee: A B Wilkie (Chester Le Street).
Attendance: 31,615

.Alex Ferguson left the League top brass grinding their teeth for the second time in a fortnight by sending out the youngest side seen on a first-team occasion at Old Trafford.

The United chief made light of the threatened £50,000 fines and fielded half-a-dozen 19-year-olds from the side that lifted the FA Youth Cup three years ago and another player aged 20. And, Fergie's Fledglings put it all in perspective, just as they had in the away leg, keeping United afloat in a cup they do not exactly covet.

Though many fans from Manchester and the Potteries gave the tie the thumbs down, those who turned up saw the quality of Old Trafford's new breed.

.In a lively opening Vale's Lee Glover, Allan Tankard and Kevin Kent all threatened to rub out that 2-1 first-leg deficit. And when defender Neil Aspin handled a cross from Keith Gillespie in the 25th minute, Nicky Butt wasted the chance to widen the aggregate difference, clipping the top of the bar with his penalty.

.It needed an old head to retrieve the situation and 30-year-old Brian McClair popped up to nod in the goal that effectively put the tie beyond Vale's reach.

When Simon Davies crossed in the 34th minute, the ball was deflected over a Vale defender by John O'Kane's flick and McClair, United's skipper for the night, headed just inside the post. Vale's efforts to stay within sight of a result were further blighted by another senior on the hour, David May scoring his first United goal. The defender rose in the box to meet a David Beckham corner and glance in United's second.

Ferguson introduced Graham Tomlinson, a £100,000 recruit from Bradford City, and Gary Neville to give them a taste of first-team work. By this time Vale, who had played with spirit before the 31,600 crowd – 1,700 of whom were travelling fans – knew it was all over.

October 8

Inside David Hirst is a man who cannot forget that Manchester United's Alex Ferguson once rated him the best English striker in these islands. The goal he scored here reminded us that at 26 there is still ample time for that judgment to be ratified.

Hirst does not have Alan Shearer's power, Matt Le Tissier's vision nor yet the sharpness of Andy Cole. But after a depressing series of injuries and surgery his quality shone again like an ingot of Sheffield steel.

He admits the fax that spelled out that £3.5 million offer from Old Trafford two years ago is something that has nagged him. When it dropped at Hillsborough the Wednesday striker, with his pace, deft control and goals, was being eyed across Europe.

What followed Wednesday's rejection was agony for Hirst, particularly as United, switching to Eric Cantona, built two championships around the Frenchman's genius.

Could he ever be the same player? Was there a chance of rekindling the interest of the biggest clubs in the game? "You're going nowhere with a really sharp knife in your ankle but you never stop thinking about things like that United offer," Hirst admitted here.

"Today's game was probably my best in two years. I can't think of another in that time that has given me as much pleasure. I was feeling a bit more like my old self. When I scored in our opening game against Spurs I said to myself 'Let's keep it rolling.'

"But nothing happened. A goal didn't come. The people around me the other lads and the manager know when I'm not myself. When I get frustrated with myself I get frustrated with other people. But now all I want is to sweep the last two years to the back of my mind."

Wednesday boss Trevor Francis had sensed that Hirst, so lethargic he had been on the subs' bench the previous three games, would spark under the challenge of United.

That goal – his fifth in nine games – against Ferguson's side showed psychology can turn plodders into performers as he scampered a couple of steps to dispatch Chris Bart-Williams' pass with his weaker right foot.

"Two years ago I would have expected him to do just what he did but on this season's form I wasn't so sure," admitted Francis.

SHEFFIELD WEDNESDAY 1
MANCHESTER UNITED 0
(Half-time score : 1-0)

Sheff Wed: Pressman, Atherton, Nolan, Hirst, Bright (Watson 89), Pearce, Bart-Williams (Taylor 65), Sheridan, Hyde, Walker, Briscoe.
United: Schmeichel, Parker (May 61), Irwin, Bruce, Sharpe, Pallister, Ince, McClair, Hughes, Keane, Gillespie (Scholes 76).
Sub: Walsh.
Scorer: Hirst 44.
Referee: P Danson (Leicester).
Attendance: 33,441

League Table After Match

	P	W	D	L	F	A	Pts
Newcastle	9	7	2	0	26	9	23
Nottm Forest	9	6	3	0	20	10	21
Blackburn	9	5	3	1	18	6	18
Liverpool	8	5	2	1	19	7	17
Man Utd	9	5	1	3	14	7	16
Chelsea	8	5	0	3	17	10	15
Southampton	9	4	3	2	14	13	15
Norwich	9	4	3	2	7	7	15
Leeds	9	4	2	3	12	10	14
Tottenham	9	4	1	4	15	17	13
Man City	9	3	3	3	14	13	12
Arsenal	9	3	2	4	11	10	11
West Ham	9	3	2	4	5	10	11
Aston Villa	9	2	3	4	10	13	9
Wimbledon	9	2	3	4	7	12	9
Sheff Wed	9	2	3	4	11	17	9
QPR	9	1	4	4	12	16	7
Ipswich	8	2	1	5	9	15	7
C Palace	9	1	4	4	6	13	7
Leicester	9	1	3	5	9	18	6
Coventry	8	1	3	4	8	18	6
Everton	9	0	3	6	7	20	3

As the ball hit the back of the net in the 43rd minute United boss Ferguson may have wondered if it was taking his hopes of a third successive title with it. Three away defeats – last season's league tally was only four – confirmed that United are scratching for the authority that sent them sailing to the Double.

There was no Cantona, Kanchelskis or Giggs, and Francis was prepared to concede that the Frenchman's absence was crucial: "He makes the difference." But though this was not in manpower or style the side who submerged Wednesday under a pile of goals to beat them four times last season Ferguson made no excuses.

Are United about to settle for the big pot at the end of their European rainbow? For two seasons no English side has been within touching distance of them. Here with Roy Keane booked for an operation and Paul Parker and Mark Hughes facing the prospect of surgery once the team is through the Champions' League stage, it looked likely.

United wasted three good first-half chances though Hughes, still the British game's most physical challenge, demanded all of Des Walker's pace and anticipation.

On the right flank young Keith Gillespie showed Hillsborough something of his neat feet before giving away to his Old Trafford kindergarten pal Paul Scholes with 14 minutes left.

John Sheridan, who orchestrated Wednesday's midfield with much assurance, insists that talk of a United title fade-out is premature. "Newcastle are bombing away at the top but United are still the team everybody has to beat. They might be a bit preoccupied with Europe but when everyone is fit again, they will be up there challenging," he said.

Schmeichel turns to see Hirst's shot go in.

October 15

Alvin Martin handed Manchester United a game they seemed incapable of winning for themselves and followed with a message Alex Ferguson, even at his stirring best, might have struggled to match.

But for one horrendous defensive slip from West Ham's hitherto old reliable, United could have been limping into Wednesday's meeting with Barcelona weak in body and spirit.

"No, they can't afford to play like that against Barcelona," agreed 36-year-old Martin, the man responsible for presenting Eric Cantona with his match-winning goal. "If they give the Spaniards the chances they gave us, then they'll be punished. But they are still a very good side.

"I look at the great Liverpool teams and say that Manchester United are in the same mould. They are as good as any side this country has sent into European competition."

It was, though, a wholly unimpressive European warm-up for United. Take away Cantona's skill and showmanship, the cutting thrust of Andrei Kanchelskis' dashing wing play, and there was not a lot to suggest United are ready to put the brakes on Newcastle's title charge.

It was just as well for United that West Ham, despite their inventive play, find goals harder to come by than tickets for Wednesday's Champions' League shindig.

In Martin Allen they had a midfielder who rivalled Cantona for man-of-the-match status. But, despite the opportunities that fell to Matthew Rush, Tony Cottee and John Moncur, the Hammers could not find a scorer.

Yet Barcelona seem to believe that it is as well to be wary. Instead of taking encouragement from what he saw, Johan Cruyff's assistant Bruins Slot viewed with apprehension the threat players like Ryan Giggs can produce.

While others saw lots of promise but too little end product from a player back in the wing business after missing a couple of games with calf trouble, Slot reasoned: "What is form with a footballer like Giggs? When you have his individuality, it's whether the luck is there that makes all the difference. He is going to be very dangerous for Barcelona. Kanchelskis is different but also dangerous."

MANCHESTER UNITED 1

WEST HAM 0

(Half-time score : 1-0)

United: Schmeichel, May (Butt 45), Irwin, Bruce, Sharpe, Pallister, Cantona, Ince, Hughes, Giggs, Kanchelskis.
Subs: McClair, Walsh.
West Ham: Miklosko, Breacker, Rowland, Potts, Martin, Allen, Marsh, Hutchison, Rush, Moncur, Cottee.
Scorer: Cantona 44.
Referee: R Gifford (Glamorgan)
Attendance: 43,795

No one could fail to be impressed with Cantona, suspension will keep him sitting in the stands on Wednesday. Slot said gratefully: "Cantona adds feeling to United. They are a different side without him. He has vision and intelligence; he's their focal point."

Ferguson, facing new injury worries about David May and Lee Sharpe, knows it, just as he knows there were too many loose ends wafting around in this untidy performance.

There is dressing-room resentment over the charge that United are now picking their games, that Europe rules their thoughts. Captain Steve Bruce said: "It's nonsense to say we are not interested in winning the championship. You can't pick and choose. We go for what is in front of us at that particular time."

Kanchelskis on the ball, looking to break the deadlock.

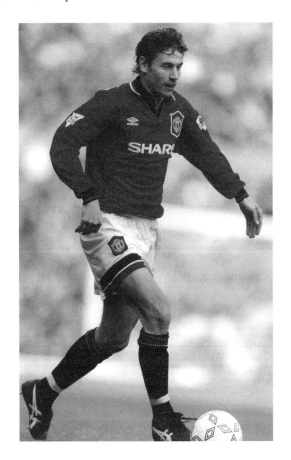

League Table After Match

	P	W	D	L	F	A	Pts
Newcastle	10	8	2	0	27	9	26
Blackburn	10	6	3	1	21	8	21
Nottm Forest	9	6	3	0	20	10	21
Man Utd	10	6	1	3	15	7	19
Liverpool	9	5	2	2	21	10	17
Norwich	10	4	4	2	8	8	16
Chelsea	9	5	0	4	18	13	15
Man City	10	4	3	3	16	14	15
Leeds	10	4	3	3	13	11	15
Southampton	10	4	3	3	17	17	15
Arsenal	10	4	2	4	14	11	14
Tottenham	10	4	2	4	16	18	14
Sheff Wed	10	3	3	4	13	18	12
Coventry	10	3	3	4	12	18	12
West Ham	10	3	2	5	5	11	11
Aston Villa	10	2	4	4	11	14	10
Wimbledon	9	2	3	4	7	12	9
Leicester	10	2	3	5	13	21	9
QPR	10	1	4	5	13	18	7
C Palace	10	1	4	5	6	14	7
Ipswich	10	2	1	7	10	19	7
Everton	10	0	3	7	7	22	3

October 19

Paul Ince took the captain's armband for United and then grabbed the tiller as one of the proudest records in European football was drifting towards the rocks.

For 38 years United have accepted all-comers to their spiritual home and none have left with victory. It was the kind of challenge Barcelona boss Johan Cruyff loves and he brought with him those deadly predators Romario and Hristo Stoichkov in a team packed with nine players who had competed in the 1994 World Cup.

With the seconds ticking away like drops of Chinese water torture United trailed 2-1 when the inspirational Ince drove forward one more time. He released a pass to Roy Keane with timing so precise it might have been measured by a computer. The Irishman glanced behind him and rolled the ball across the area for Lee Sharpe to score a marvellous goal that brought a crescendo from the enthralled 40,064 crowd left breathless by the action-packed match.

Alex Ferguson had said that United must take something from every Champions' League match this season and that goal secured the point that may yet prove critical in the tight Group A.

We had been promised a contest that would entertain but the football soared above all expectations.

Ryan Giggs was unable to take part because of ankle ligament damage, five other United players nursed injuries and Frenchman Eric Cantona was still banned. Ferguson gambled. He dropped skipper Steve Bruce, fearing Romario's pace against him, and put Paul Parker in as a man-to-man marker.

It looked like a losing throw of the dice when Jose-Maria Bakero gave the Spaniards the lead just after half-time. But Ince postponed inquests on the Bruce decision by refusing to accept defeat. He exemplified the spirit of United and inspired others around him to play their full part in a thrilling game.

Sharpe took the Giggs role and terrorised Luis Martinez in the first half while on the other flank Andrei Kanchelskis bewildered Sergi with his pace. There was young Nicky Butt, maturing in European ties, and there was Mark Hughes playing against his former club after a couple of unhappy years there.

MANCHESTER UNITED 2

BARCELONA 2

(Half-time score : 1-1)

United: Schmeichel, Parker, Irwin, May (Bruce 69), Butt (Scholes 66), Pallister, Kanchelskis, Ince, Keane, Hughes, Sharpe.
Sub: Walsh.
Barcelona: Busquets, Abelardo, Guardiola, Koeman, Sergi, Bakero, Luis, Martinez (Sacristan 45), Stoichkov, Nadal, Romario, Baguiristain (Jordi 67)
Scorers: (United): Hughes 18, Sharpe 80; (Barcelona): Romario 34, Bakero 49.
Referee: I Craciunescu (Romania).
Attendance: 40,064

It was Hughes, destroyer of Barcelona in the 1991 Cup Winner's Cup final, who opened the scoring in the 19th minute. Sharpe, despite his good all-round play, had previously delivered some disappointing crosses but he was inch-perfect this time and Hughes met it at the far post with a powerful header.

Meanwhile there were worries at the back. Without Bruce United were neither composed nor organised and in the 34th minute they were caught waiting for an offside decision when Ronald Koeman and Bakero combined to send Romario through. The flag stayed down and the brilliant Brazilian drove the ball through Peter Schmeichel's legs as the goalkeeper came to meet him.

Worse followed four minutes into the second half as United's defenders stood around like a group of pensioners discussing the weather. Bakero chested down Koeman's 50-yard pass and drove the ball home. United's composure was in threads. It seemed their 55th tie at home in Europe would lead to their first defeat. Ince, though, would have none of it.

Indeed Paul Scholes, a 66th-minute substitute for Butt, almost gave United victory in the 90th minute when he chipped Carlos Busquets, only to see the ball dip just over the bar.

Lee Sharpe scores to keep United in the game.

October 23

United got by with a little help from an unlikely friend at Ewood Park – referee Gerald Ashby.

It is tough enough taking on the champions with a full quota of players but the dismissal of Rovers' full-back Henning Berg halfway through this duel in driving rain changed the balance. United did not need a second invitation to narrow the gap between themselves and Newcastle to seven points as they moved into third place.

United were huffing and puffing for most of a frenetic first half during which the well of strong feeling between the two clubs bubbled like a boiling kettle. On a surface shimmering with rain the timing of tackles was never going to be easy but the one that swung the pendulum of play carried as much malice as a feather duster.

Lee Sharpe was the victim, as he had been when Norwegian Berg got his first caution 10 minutes earlier. Ashby, though, saw it as unfair, awarded a penalty and produced the red card.

Until that moment United had looked as if the tiredness from their heroic game against Barcelona was still stiffening their limbs. Blackburn, in belligerent mood, sensed that Ferguson's men, who had come into the game on the back of three successive away defeats, were there for the taking.

Rovers dispensed with the sparring after 13 minutes and landed the big punch. Peter Schmeichel had a typical rush of blood to the head and raced out to Graeme Le Saux's free-kick. But he could manage only a weak fist-out and the ball fell to Paul Warhurst who, from 30 yards, lifted it back over his head and into the net.

Steve Bruce, Chris Sutton and Berg had all been shown yellow cards when referee Ashby made his decisive intervention. As Berg trooped off disbelievingly Eric Cantona stroked home the penalty with his usual arrogance.

Blackburn were forced to retreat, withdrawing Sutton to central defence and replacing Berg with Warhurst at right-back. Yet they reclaimed the lead in the 51st minute when Colin Hendry headed home from Jason Wilcox's cross.

Within a minute United were level again as Andrei Kanchelskis drove across a centre which Hendry tried to clear. It fell again for the

BLACKBURN 2
MANCHESTER UNITED 4
(Half-time score : 1-1)

Blackburn: Flowers, Gale (Pearce 84), Hendry, Le Saux, Ripley, Shearer, Wilcox, Sutton, Berg, Atkins (Slater 84), Warhurst.
United: Schmeichel, Irwin, Bruce, Sharpe, Pallister, Cantona, Ince, Hughes, Kanchelskis, Keane, Butt (McClair 82).
Subs: Gillespie, Walsh.
Scorers: (Blackburn): Warhurst 13, Hendry 51; (United): Cantona 45 pen, Kanchelskis 52, 82, Hughes 67.
Referee: G Ashby (Worcester).
Attendance: 30,260

	P	W	D	L	F	A	Pts
Newcastle............	11	9	2	0	29	10	29
Nottm Forest.....	11	8	3	0	25	11	27
Man Utd.............	11	7	1	3	19	9	22
Blackburn...........	11	6	3	2	23	12	21
Liverpool..........	10	6	2	2	24	10	20
Norwich..............	11	5	4	2	12	10	19
Chelsea...............	10	6	0	4	20	13	18
Man City............	11	5	3	3	21	16	18
Arsenal...............	11	5	2	4	16	12	17
Leeds..................	10	4	3	3	13	11	15
Southampton.....	11	4	3	4	17	19	15
West Ham...........	11	4	2	5	7	11	14
Tottenham..........	11	4	2	5	18	23	14
Sheff Wed...........	11	3	3	5	14	20	12
Coventry............	11	3	3	5	13	20	12
Aston Villa........	11	2	4	5	11	16	10
C Palace.............	11	2	4	5	7	14	10
Leicester.............	10	2	3	5	13	21	9
Wimbledon.........	11	2	3	6	8	18	9
QPR....................	11	1	4	6	15	22	7
Ipswich...............	11	2	1	8	10	21	7
Everton..............	11	0	3	8	7	23	3

Ukrainian and he shot ferociously into the far corner. It was as if a smooth saloon had suddenly suffered a blow out. Rovers slithered to a crawl and Paul Ince once again took control.

Now, instead of playing their football in front of the Blackburn defence, United were achieving penetration. The more possession they gained the weaker 10-man Blackburn became.

It must have been tormenting for Rovers, who had taken four points from the champions last season, yet they contributed to their own downfall as United took the lead for the first time. Le Saux gave the ball away to Mark Hughes as he tried to pass inside and, with Tim Flowers stranded off his line, the Welsh striker lifted the ball over him with wonderful skill to make it 3-2.

Rovers were forced to push forward, leaving gaps for Cantona, Kanchelskis and Ince to drive into. Kanchelskis was not going to be denied a second goal and, with eight minutes left, he collected Sharpe's pass and ran the length of the Blackburn half before waltzing past Flowers to score.

Shearer looks on as Schmeichel executes a superb save from Stuart Ripley's shot.

October 26

Philippe Albert, the straight-backed Belgian with the guardsman's gait, applied the bayonet to the reserve side that Manchester United sent to Newcastle last night.

A flock of Fergie fledglings, including five teenagers, had spread their wings at St James' Park and Kevin Keegan's side had looked increasingly frustrated. There were only eight minutes left when Swiss international Marc Hottiger crossed from the right and Albert soared to score his first goal for the club. With the breakthrough achieved and United committed to seek an equaliser, Paul Kitson helped himself to his first goal since moving to the club from Derby County.

This was a result that truly suited both parties. Ferguson has made no secret of the fact he viewed the Coca-Cola Cup as an inhibition to his European Cup and Premier League ambitions. He made the right noises after the game when he said: "We don't like to lose any game but, if we are going to do well in other tournaments this season, we have to spread our staff a bit.

"It was difficult for Newcastle because they had expected me to play the older players. I hope they go on to do well because they have been a breath of fresh air this season. They have played their football the right way."

It was a night for mutual respect as Keegan was ready to offer his own praise about the quality of the youngsters Fergie has unveiled. "When you looked at the line-ups it seemed they were fielding a side we might overrun," said Keegan. "But they have some very good youngsters and we had to fight all the way."

For United there was still a price to pay for this absorbing, exciting and competitive game. Lee Sharpe, who came on as a second-half substitute, is out of Saturday's Premier League meeting between the sides at Old Trafford. Denis Irwin, the man he replaced, has a knee injury and Nicky Butt also finished the game limping with knee trouble, a worrying situation for the club with Barcelona to face next week.

Ferguson's concern must have been offset by the mature performances he received in midfield from Butt and the impressive David Beckham while Keith Gillespie looks as if he could stand in if Sharpe

NEWCASTLE 2
MANCHESTER UNITED 0
(Half-time score : 0-0)

Newcastle: Srnicek, Hottiger, Beresford, Howey, Peacock, Albert, Beardsley, Watson, Sellars, Cole (Guppy 63), Kitson.
United: Walsh, Neville, Irwin (Sharpe 51), Bruce, Butt, Pallister, Gillespie, Beckham, McClair, Scholes, Davies.
Subs: Pilkington, Tomlinson.
Scorers: Albert 82, Kitson 87.
Referee: T Holbrook (Walsall).
Attendance: 34,178

and Ryan Giggs are ruled out.

Newcastle will not lose many games in their splendid citadel, once again bulging with a crowd of 34,178 inside, and this victory, their 18th consecutive unbeaten match, sets a record.

They play their football with a refreshing, open style and but for the courageous defending of Steve Bruce in the opening 15 minutes, this contest might not have been in suspense for so long.

With Peter Beardsley endlessly probing, Scott Sellars looking like a marathon runner and Kitson anxious to prove his muscular pedigree there was bound to come a time when the United kids would weaken.

Albert's jubilation at scoring his first goal fitted the festival atmosphere in the night air. "I'm pleased for him because he has had to play in just about every position except the one I bought him for," said Keegan. "And I was pleased to see Kitson get his first goal because he is a very exciting lad."

Philippe Albert heading in Newcastle's opener.

October 29

It was not so much a game of football as an eloquent statement of intent, laced with superlatives and stunningly persuasive in the message that it is dangerous to mess with Manchester United.

The question posed – no sleaze money required – was whether Newcastle United were serious pretenders to the seat of power in the Premiership. Kevin Keegan's side were chastened by the response.

They had crossed the Pennines hoping to return with a 10-point advantage on the champions. Now they must look over their shoulders at the pursuing pack, a mere six points separating first from fifth.

Managers tend to assess games on a scale of one to three, depending on the number of points collected. Just occasionally they leave empty-handed but full of heart.

Keegan is an optimist and ambassador, too. His disappointment at seeing a marvellous unbeaten 18-match run concluded was offset by the knowledge that his side had richly contributed to a contest of epic entertainment.

"It was a terrific game," he said. "The pace of it took your breath away. Great atmosphere. Great surface. Great players. Wrong result. The consolation for me is that we have come here and played them the way we wanted to play them. We have showed some character. But they are good everybody knows that.

"Whoever wins the league has to beat them. I have been saying that every week so I am not going to say any different having lost here. In the last 25 minutes, when they were 2-0 up, they were exceptional. At that stage the one thing you want as opposition manager is for the match to start going a bit quicker and get it over with."

Without the injured Andy Cole and Paul Kitson, and against a mean defence, it would have been easy for Keegan to stock up midfield and try to stall the opposition. That, though, would have been a betrayal of his commitment to make the game an appealing spectacle.

He knew the champions are most comfortable against teams that come at them because they can then maximise the pace of their forwards, especially winger Andrei Kanchelskis.

Newcastle took the gamble and paid the price. But in the meantime they enhanced their reputation as a side of genuine adventure. It

MANCHESTER UNITED 2
NEWCASTLE 0
(Half-time score : 1-0)

United: Schmeichel, Keane, Irwin, Bruce, Kanchelskis, Pallister, Cantona, Ince, McClair, Hughes, Giggs (Gillespie 66).
Subs: Butt, Walsh.
Newcastle: Srnicek, Hottiger (Mathie 75), Beresford, Albert, Peacock, Howey, Watson, Beardsley, Lee, Fox (Clark 75), Sellars.
Scorers: Pallister 11, Gillespie 77.
Referee: J B Worrall (Warrington).
Attendance: 43,795

should surprise nobody that the gates are locked each time they play.

That has been the case with Manchester United for some years now and the week just gone proved a good one victories over Blackburn and Newcastle in the Premiership and an honourable exit from the Coca-Cola Cup with the kids coming of age.

As they brace themselves for Barcelona, Ferguson has the reassurance that his defence has been tested sternly in readiness for what lies in store in the Nou Camp on Wednesday.

"I knew Newcastle would try to beat us," he said. "So often teams come here just to frustrate us and when that happens you tend not to have to sweat too much defensively. Newcastle make you sweat. Some of their last-third play is excellent, one-touch football around the edge of the area and you really have to be alert to it."

There was some fine interplay between Robert Lee and Peter Beardsley but the test would have been stiffer with Cole on the end of it and Keegan admitted: "We were a toothless tiger and never really had the penetration we normally have.

"I think if Alex lost Mark Hughes he would have a problem up front. There are not many of those type around: Cole, Hughes, Ferdinand, Wright, Shearer, Sutton. That's why people pay 5m for them.

"United really do break at pace but they like teams to come at them and we didn't let them down. Barcelona's Johan Cruyff has a similar attitude to me. He was a forward. What the hell do we know about defending? Go out and have a crack. You don't have players like Romario and Stoichkov and defend."

With Paul Ince moving through the gears like Damon Hill and Kanchelskis showing the pace that would make him favourite in the Greyhound Derby, United were a spectacle to behold.

"Some of our attacking play was magnificent," said Ferguson. "I think Pavel Srnicek has probably had his best-ever game. He has been excellent.

"The pace of our play was a great advert for the game. We tend to overlook that factor. When you see tremendous skills exhibited at that speed then you get the excitement."

Young Ulsterman Keith Gillespie, a replacement after an hour for a muted Ryan Giggs, scored a goal which served only to underline the richness of the seam at Old Trafford. That, perhaps, is the difference between the champions and the pretenders. No Cole, no goal. United, on the other hand, are spreading the goalscoring load.

Yet Fergie has his own headache now: that of selecting the side to face Barcelona. He says he will bring Paul Parker in at right-back and move Roy Keane, who played well there in this game, into midfield.

If he plays Peter Schmeichel, Denis Irwin and Keane, however, Giggs will have to sit it out. It is the old game of musical chairs. He must hope the music he plays it to has the same high notes it reached here.

Paul Ince is confronted by the Newcastle defenders, Steve Howey and Darren Peacock.

League Table After Match

	P	W	D	L	F	A	Pts
Newcastle	12	9	2	1	29	12	29
Nottm Forest	12	8	3	1	25	13	27
Man Utd	12	8	1	3	21	9	25
Blackburn	12	7	3	2	25	12	24
Liverpool	11	7	2	2	27	11	23
Leeds	12	6	3	3	18	13	21
Chelsea	11	6	1	4	21	14	19
Norwich	12	5	4	3	12	11	19
Man City	12	5	3	4	21	17	18
Arsenal	12	5	3	4	17	13	18
Tottenham	12	5	2	5	21	24	17
Southampton	12	4	3	5	18	22	15
Coventry	12	4	3	5	14	20	15
West Ham	12	4	2	6	8	14	14
Sheff Wed	12	3	4	5	15	21	13
C Palace	12	3	4	5	8	14	13
Wimbledon	12	3	3	6	9	18	12
QPR	12	2	4	6	17	22	10
Aston Villa	12	2	4	6	11	18	10
Leicester	12	2	3	7	14	24	9
Ipswich	12	2	1	9	11	24	7
Everton	12	0	4	8	8	24	4

November 2

BARCELONA 4
MANCHESTER UNITED 0
(Half-time score : 2-0)

Barcelona: Busquets, Ferrer, Guardiola, Koeman, Abelardo, Bakero (Sanchez Jara 77), Amor, Stoichkov, Cruyff (Ivan Iglesias 63), Romario, Sergi.
United: Walsh, Parker, Bruce, Pallister, Irwin, Kanchelskis, Ince, Keane, Butt, Giggs (Scholes 80), Hughes.
Scorers: Pallister 9 og, Romario 45, Stoichkov 52, Ferrer 88.
Referee: J Quiniou (France).
Attendance: 115,000

Hristo Stoichkov, Barcelona's barrel-chested Bulgarian, performed a personal demolition job on the reputation of Manchester United and the status of English football. The man who deposed Germany in the World Cup last summer addressed his artistry to Alex Ferguson's high fliers and brought them crashing to earth.

United have to turn back the clock almost 15 years to find a European defeat as comprehensive as this one, a 4-0 reverse against Porto.

Ferguson dropped Danish keeper Peter Schmeichel to accommodate Ryan Giggs, another questionable European gamble that failed to produce a winning hand. With Gothenburg beating Galatasaray 1-0 in Turkey, Ferguson knows United must win in Sweden in three weeks' time and defeat the Turks at home to be certain of a quarter-final place.

The fact that Eric Cantona will be back for the final two Champions' League games is a crumb of consolation.

It is a sobering thought that Barcelona's Mean Machine cost a collective £5.5 million, more or less the price of Chris Sutton, which puts the English transfer market into perspective. Barcelona also threw a harsh light on the standard of English football. Rarely have the elite of the domestic game been subjected to quite such a mauling.

Ferguson's theory was that this huge, wide pitch was the breeding ground for an assault down the wings, so effective at Old Trafford. But Barcelona's Albert Ferrer was back after injury to hold one flank while on the other Sergi, on home soil, was not about to allow the chasing he had from Andrei Kanchelskis in Manchester.

So what had been a profitable area of attack was now a cul-de-sac and you could count on one hand the crosses fired into the Spanish penalty area.

That nullified the threat of Nou Camp old boy Mark Hughes, whose memories of Barcelona are far from happy ones. Stoichkov scored twice, laid on one for Romario and made the significant contribution to what Ferguson described as his most humiliating experience at United.

Romario, of course, is an extraordinary player, and Gary Pallister learned that sometimes football is conducted on a higher plane than he has yet experienced. The squat Brazilian has a panther-like pace and an instinct for space that makes him almost impossible to mark. Here, for sure, is one of the great players in the game.

United's defence leaked like a holed ship and the Spaniards chased into the empty spaces like men on the loot. For boss Johan Cruyff and the 115,000 Catalan fans filling the steep banks of this majestic stadium it was a night of celebration.

When the statistics are viewed they show that United never managed a shot on goal which, for a side famed for their prolific scoring, makes sobering reading. The damage started in the ninth minute with a goal of some fortune. Bakero's initial shot was cleared by Ince but the ball was squared by Jordi Cruyff to Stoichkov, whose shot deflected off Pallister into the net.

Stoichkov swaggered almost lazily down the right on the stroke of half-time before delivering the perfect cross on to Romario's chest. In one movement he controlled it and swept imperiously past a static, stunned Pallister before driving his shot through Gary Walsh's legs.

United were forced to chase the game, just what Romario and Stoichkov relished. The Bulgarian made a mesmerising run in the 52nd minute, took a return ball off Romario's heel and drove it in.

Even the discipline suffered, Ince and Parker being booked in the space of a couple of minutes for dissent. Full-back Ferrer made it four in the 88th minute, drifting past Kanchelskis and cashing in on a rebound off the shell-shocked Pallister.

There is still the chance of recovery but United will carry the wound of this defeat through the months ahead and realise that beyond our shores there is a world of football with another dimension.

November 6

ASTON VILLA 1

MANCHESTER UNITED 2

(Half-time score : 1-1)

Villa: Spink, Barrett, Staunton (Yorke 58), Ehiogu, McGrath, Richardson, Houghton (Parker 79), King, Saunders, Atkinson, Townsend.
United: Walsh, Kanchelskis, Irwin, Bruce, Keane, Pallister, Cantona, Ince, Butt (McClair 7), Scholes (Gillespie 79), Giggs.
Sub: Pilkington.
Scorers: (Villa): Bruce 29 og; (United): Ince 44, Kanchelskis 51.
Referee: P Don (Middlesex).
Attendance: 32,136

It took time, as bad hangovers tend to, but United eventually found the cure for the deadly, heady cocktail of Stoichkov and Romario.

A victory that could not be classed as decisive keeps United in touch with Newcastle and the championship, which might be just as well after what we witnessed in Barcelona.

It was earned at the expense of a Villa side deep in relegation trouble, yet playing as if they should be challenging at the other end of the table. If Chairman Doug Ellis is as knowledgeable on the game as he boasts, he will cut the cackle about the jeopardy of Ron Atkinson's position as manager and get behind him.

He might also use his voice as an FA councillor to call for some consistency from referees after Villa were denied what looked a clear penalty four minutes from time.

Ellis, of course, can call up some chilling statistics: seven defeats in Villa's last eight games and only 18 points from 21 Premiership matches since they defeated United in the Coca-Cola Cup final last March. Yet United owed victory in the end to Gary Walsh, deputising for the injured Peter Schmeichel, for two wonderful fingertip saves which compensated for his nervousness at crosses.

Critical to United was the loss of Mark Hughes, whose strength and ability to hold up the ball are such a huge influence.

The champions are presently betraying their reputation partly because Frenchman Eric Cantona seems to have dropped his baton in the orchestra pit. There has been a lack of rhythm to their game. You would have thought they might have learned their lesson about passing and keeping the ball at the Nou Camp, but apparently not.

The forceful Steve Staunton should have scored for Villa after 58 seconds when a bad back-pass was scooped to his feet by the scrambling Walsh, but Staunton struck his shot wide of an unguarded net.

United were unfortunate to lose Nicky Butt in the seventh minute after a clash of heads with Ugo Ehiogu, bringing on Brian McClair. A more general problem was that too many players in midfield, Paul Ince and Cantona among them, were standing with hands on hips when possession was lost. The attitude allowed Villa to go ahead in the 29th minute.

Dalian Atkinson, who has not scored in the Premiership since last January 1, will claim the goal but it was Steve Bruce's boot that deflected his 25-yard shot over Walsh's head. United were fortunate that their dilatory posing did not cost them another goal in the 38th minute when Staunton strode forward to strike a superb shot which had Walsh swallow-diving to keep it out.

The break United needed came a minute before half-time, courtesy of indecision from Andy Townsend. Ehiogu's headed clearance of an Andrei Kanchelskis centre bounced twice while Ince geared himself for a shot and Townsend hesitated. When Ince's boot finally connected, the ball flew home.

Six minutes into the second half United completed their rehabilitation. Denis Irwin's cross from the left carried past the dummying Cantona to Kanchelskis who drove the ball through Phil King's legs and into the net.

Staunton left the action clutching his shoulder and Dwight Yorke came on and sent Walsh into another acrobatic save. Then Bruce put an out-stretched arm across Paul McGrath in a packed penalty area, but World Cup referee Philip Don, a few yards from the incident, refused to give what looked an obvious penalty.

It was a cruel finale for Villa, typical of their luck at the moment. If they continue to unearth this fighting spirit, the results will surely come. But as manager Atkinson said: "People will be calling for a change of personnel now, whether it be the players or me. The parasites will be coming out of the woodwork. One point from eight games is a disaster."

League Table After Match

	P	W	D	L	F	A	Pts
Newcastle	13	10	2	1	31	13	32
Blackburn	14	9	3	2	28	12	30
Man Utd	13	9	1	3	23	10	28
Nottm Forrest	13	8	3	2	25	14	27
Liverpool	13	8	2	3	29	13	26
Leeds	14	7	3	4	21	16	24
Norwich	14	5	6	3	13	12	21
Chelsea	12	6	2	4	23	16	20
Man City	13	5	4	4	24	20	19
Arsenal	13	5	4	4	17	13	19
C Palace	14	5	4	5	15	15	19
Southampton	14	4	5	5	22	26	17
Tottenham	13	5	2	6	21	26	17
West Ham	14	5	2	7	9	15	17
Coventry	14	4	4	6	17	26	16
Sheff Wed	14	3	5	6	15	22	14
QPR	14	3	4	7	20	25	13
Wimbledon	13	3	3	7	10	21	12
Aston Villa	13	2	4	7	12	20	10
Ipswich	14	3	1	10	13	27	10
Leicester	13	2	3	8	14	25	9
Everton	14	1	5	8	9	24	8

November 10

MANCHESTER UNITED 5

MANCHESTER CITY 0

(Half-time score : 2-0)

United: Schmeichel, Keane, Irwin, Bruce, Kanchelskis, Pallister, Cantona, Ince, McClair, Hughes, Giggs (Scholes 45).
Subs: Neville, Walsh.
City: Tracey, Edghill, Phelan, I. Brightwell, Summerbee, Vonk, Lomas, Walsh, Quinn, Flitcroft, Beagrie.
Scorers: Cantona 24, Kanchelskis 43, 47, 88, Hughes 70.
Referee: K Cooper (Pontypridd).
Attendance: 43,738

Andrei Kanchelskis turned on the turbo-charger and City scattered in blind panic as he went joy-riding among their defenders. He left a pile of blue-shirted debris strewn across Old Trafford and up on Tyneside you sensed that Newcastle United could hear the roar of the approaching engine.

United's annihilation of their neighbours brought them to within two points of the Carling Premiership leaders and suddenly the old confidence and swagger were back. Barcelona seemed a distant, dark cloud as Kanchelskis, Cantona and Co responded to the driving inspiration of Paul Ince to put City's revival into perspective.

For, if the Ukrainian initiated the first goal and scored a hat-trick, Ince dominated the midfield and made sure City were unable to build. But Ince, who received a magnum of champagne as Carling's Player of October before the game, goes into hospital today for a sinus operation and is doubtful for England's match with Nigeria on Wednesday.

This was United's biggest victory in 121 derby games and City looked fragile in defence with Tony Coton, Andy Dibble and Keith Curle absent. Cantona and Kanchelskis combined first to pick the lock, then to kick the door open. The opening goal was a foretaste as Kanchelskis lifted the perfect pass forward, Cantona caught it on his heel, flicked it forward and thumped it home.

There should have been a second a few minutes later when Roy Keane, looking an accomplished right-back, ventured forward on to Cantona's measured pass and Simon Tracey did well to stop the shot.

It was almost half-time before City were certain of their destiny. Cantona had Ian Brightwell and Terry Phelan scuttling backwards desperately laying the ball off to Kanchelskis and, though he was fortunate his shot deflected off Phelan's heel, the goal was deserved.

After that it was a procession. Ryan Giggs gave way for Paul Scholes but he had merely a walk-on role as the triangle of Ince, Cantona and Kanchelskis went on the rampage.

Two minutes into the second half a Cantona back-header sent Kanchelskis on a dazzling cross-field run. The initial shot hit Tracey but the ball came back off him and the Ukrainian made it three.

City flickered briefly as Pallister deflected a Paul Walsh shot over the bar from inside the six-yard box but at the other end Mark Hughes, colliding with Michel Vonk as both went for a Keane cross, recovered his balance brilliantly to steer home the loose ball.

The record-breaking goal came two minutes from time – Cantona on the break, Kanchelskis waiting in the middle and again a finish at the second attempt.

United boss Alex Ferguson said: "At times in the second half some of our football was absolutely magnificent. This was a real Eric Cantona show."

Kanchelskis, in his still faltering English, said: "I like Manchester. They very good side." Every word was true.

League Table After Match

	P	W	D	L	F	A	Pts
Newcastle	14	10	3	1	31	13	33
Man Utd	14	10	1	3	28	10	31
Blackburn	14	9	3	2	28	12	30
Liverpool	14	9	2	3	32	14	29
Nottm Forest	14	8	4	2	25	14	28
Leeds	14	7	3	4	21	16	24
Norwich	14	5	6	3	13	12	21
Chelsea	13	6	2	5	24	19	20
Arsenal	13	5	4	4	17	13	19
C Palace	14	5	4	5	15	15	19
Man City	14	5	4	5	24	25	19
Southampton	14	4	5	5	22	26	17
Tottenham	13	5	2	6	21	26	17
West Ham	14	5	2	7	9	15	17
Coventry	14	4	4	6	17	26	16
Wimbledon	14	4	3	7	14	24	15
Sheff Wed	14	3	5	6	15	22	14
QPR	14	3	4	7	20	25	13
Aston Villa	14	2	4	8	15	24	10
Ipswich	14	3	1	10	13	27	10
Leicester	13	2	3	8	14	25	9
Everton	14	1	5	8	9	24	8

Kanchelskis strikes home United's second out of five.

November 19

MANCHESTER UNITED 3

CRYSTAL PALACE 0

(Half-time score : 2-0)

United: Schmeichel (Pilkington 8), Neville, Irwin, May, Davies (Scholes 71), Pallister, Cantona, Ince, McClair, Hughes, Kanchelskis (Gillespie 52).).
Palace: Martyn, Humphrey, Gordon, Southgate, Shaw, Coleman, Patterson (Bowry 69), Newman, Armstrong, Preece, Salako.
Scorers: Irwin 8, Cantona 34, Kanchelskis 50.
Referee: B Hill (Market Harborough).
Attendance: 43,788

Crystal Palace boss Alan Smith has no doubt about it: Eric Cantona will frighten Swedish champions Gothenburg to death this week. Forget the fissures in the stricken United side Alex Ferguson takes over the North Sea tomorrow. Smith believes the greatest player operating in the British Isles will rescue them.

On the day United galloped ahead of the Premiership pack, Ferguson had showed Old Trafford the young legs and lungs that will almost certainly drive his club into the 21st century.

Deputy keeper Kevin Pilkington, Gary Neville, Simon Davies, Keith Gillespie and Nicky Butt are all Gothenburg-bound. But Smith insists Cantona, in his first European match of the season, has the Scandinavians running scared.

"Physically he's way above everyone else in our game," said the Palace boss. "Of course Eric is technically brilliant. But his physical presence is enormous. I often tell my players to set their stall out by this man. He is in a class of his own in British football. I can't think of anyone even vaguely like him in these islands. He's a unique type of player.

"You have got to be a bold manager to assimilate him in your side. You certainly wouldn't do it if you were a system manager. I don't think Gothenburg will have anyone to match him. I've seen them three times this season on trips to watch players and I believe they will be frightened to death by Cantona. He's special.

"Andrei Kanchelskis has terrific pace but still has an obvious sort of playing style. Giggs has his tricks. But Cantona, with his power and technical brilliance, has developed almost a mystique about his play."

Against such an opponent any side needs luck at Fortress Old Trafford, and Palace were out of it. United should have had Denis Irwin sent off after 22 minutes for illegally stopping Chris Armstrong on route for goal, and young debutant Pilkington could easily have gone soon afterwards.

Old Trafford's third-choice keeper, arriving after seven minutes in place of the injured Peter Schmeichel, clearly handled outside the box, though he could plead his momentum carried him there. But Brian Hill, an ostrich in referee's garb, did not even reach for a card.

Palace fans were still bellowing "cheat" at the official when Cantona's forehead met Kanchelskis' superbly placed cross for 2-0. There was no way back for Palace. Irwin had already thundered a free-kick in off their defensive wall. Kanchelskis was to add a third off the inside of Nigel Martyn's near post: game, set and match.

Manager Smith would not cite the referee's inconsistency as a reason for the end of Palace's five-match winning streak, though two of his players were booked for less obvious offences than Irwin's and Pilkington's.

Alongside Cantona's control and the flank play of Kanchelskis there were fine cameos from Fergie's fledglings. Pilkington kept his cool despite that one misdemeanour and Simon Davies operated on the wing usually monopolised by Sharpe and Giggs with conviction before giving way to Scholes.

But in the right-back role released by Paul Parker he has an operation today Gary Neville was a revelation. His superbly assured show made him a contender for the regular No 2 shirt though David May – a centre-back replacement here for the suspended Steve Bruce – will probably get the job in Sweden.

The win prolonged United's remarkable success at Old Trafford – eight wins from eight Premiership games this season for a 20-0 goal difference.

"It would be good for British football if they beat Gothenburg and, if the Swedes make the same mistakes as us, they will," said Smith. "But we took a bit of credit out of the exercise. I still think I've a good team and they shouldn't lose confidence from this one result."

League Table After Match

	P	W	D	L	F	A	Pts
Man Utd	15	11	1	3	31	10	34
Blackburn	15	10	3	2	31	13	33
Newcastle	15	10	3	2	33	16	33
Liverpool	14	9	2	3	32	14	29
Nottm Forest	15	8	4	3	25	15	28
Leeds	15	7	3	5	23	19	24
Chelsea	14	7	2	5	25	19	23
Man City	15	6	4	5	25	25	22
Norwich	15	5	6	4	13	13	21
Southampton	15	5	5	5	23	26	20
Arsenal	14	5	4	5	17	14	19
C Palace	15	5	4	6	15	18	19
Coventry	15	5	4	6	18	26	19
Wimbledon	15	5	3	7	17	26	18
Tottenham	14	5	2	7	24	30	17
Sheff Wed	15	4	5	6	16	22	17
West Ham	15	5	2	8	9	16	17
QPR	15	4	4	7	23	27	16
Aston Villa	15	3	4	8	19	27	13
Ipswich	15	3	1	11	14	30	10
Leicester	14	2	3	9	14	26	9
Everton	14	1	5	8	9	24	8

November 23

IFK GOTHENBURG 3

MANCHESTER UNITED 1

(Half-time score : 1-0)

Gothenburg: Ravelli, Kamark, Johansson, Bjorklund, Nilsson, Martinsson (Wahlstedt 48), Erlingmark, Lindqvist, Blomqvist, Rehn, Pettersson (Andersson 78).
United: Walsh, May (Neville 68), Irwin, Bruce, Kanchelskis, Pallister, Cantona, Ince, McClair, Hughes, Davies (Butt 75).
Scorers: (IFK): Blomqvist 10, Erlingmark 64, Kamark 71 pen; (United): Hughes 64.
Referee: A Trentalange (Italy).
Attendance: 36,350

Alex Ferguson criticised his defence and wrote off Manchester United's European Cup chances after they crashed in Gothenburg.

Paul Ince was sent off for dissent as United were humiliatingly beaten by the Swedes in the Champions' League Group A. They now need a miracle to reach the quarter-finals.

"We just weren't good enough," said Ferguson. "You can use all sorts of excuses but at the end of the night we were well beaten."

United's only hope, after Barcelona slumped to a last-minute defeat to Galatasaray, is that United beat the Turks in two weeks while the Spanish champions lose to Gothenburg. But Ferguson holds out little hope. And he criticised his defence for not learning from the lessons of the 4-0 defeat in Barcelona earlier this month.

"I think we are out," he said. "We are capable of beating anyone at Old Trafford but what is important is that Barcelona have to lose at home and I can't see that happening. The defeat hurts me more than the one against Barcelona because this was the night when the chips were down and I am so terribly disappointed in our performance."

Ferguson was particularly upset at the way United's defence crumbled again so that, in two matches, the total of goals that have flown past poor Gary Walsh reached seven.

Ferguson insisted: "We had worked hour upon hour on what happened in Barcelona but we were guilty again of some dreadful defending. It is hard to believe we could lose the kind of goals we did. As in Barcelona we were guilty of terrible defending."

When the inquests are held on this night of distress it will doubtless be claimed that Uefa's inhibiting foreign rule has been a fatal disruption to United's hopes. Ferguson has had the worry beads out each time he has made a European team selection and, as long as he is denied the services of some of his first choices, there are always going to be difficulties matching the deeds of the United team of 1968 who carried off the European Cup so gloriously at Wembley.

On this rainswept night, with a difficult swirling wind and a pitch that would pose problems for a Land-Rover, United never hinted at the form that has swept them through the last two seasons. Just as they were shredded by Barcelona earlier this month, so United were subjected to the roller-coaster treatment from Sweden stars Jesper Blomqvist and Stefan Pettersson.

No one suffered more than poor David May, who looked as if he was playing football in a maze. Wherever he turned there was trouble and when he was withdrawn in the second half it was an act of mercy.

The absence of Peter Schmeichel surely had some bearing on the jitters that afflicted the United defence. Reserve team football is no preparation for a goalkeeper to face world-class forwards, as Walsh discovered.

The problems were not restricted to the defence. There was a lack of drive from midfield, no measured passing from Brian McClair and none of those surging runs into the box from Ince.

Perhaps too much had been expected of Eric Cantona, who was meant to lead United from the wilderness but guided them only into a desert. Certainly there was no sign of that regal arrogance in the face of some aggressive and concerted Swedish defending which drew United on for the lightning counter-attack.

Gothenburg have a strong European pedigree. They have lost only twice at home in 39 matches since 1979. These are the same players we appreciated in Sweden's World Cup team in America last summer. Seasoned and slick, they were quickly away from the starting stalls in their pursuit of a victory that ensured their quarter-final place.

May's catalogue of misfortune began in the second minute with a foul on the quicksilver Blomqvist. When Hughes encroached as the kick was taken he got a booking that put him out of the Galatasaray game.

As if that was not enough, United were a goal down in the 10th minute, caught square and looking in vain for an offside flag as, Blomqvist took a return pass from Stefan Rehn and ran on to score. The camera showed that Denis Irwin had not stepped forward in unison as the pass was played.

United might have been on equal terms in the 16th minute when a Gary Pallister free-kick fell to Andrei Kanchelskis. But veteran goalkeeper Thomas Ravelli, now in his 36th year, was at him like a cobra.

Cantona's frustration surfaced with a yellow card at the start of the second half for a lunge at Joachim Bjorklund.

Then, suddenly United found a lifeline. May produced one of his few quality balls into the box, Cantona flicked it forward neatly and Hughes finished it off.

There was no excuse when, a minute later, United were caught out. May was left for dead along the by-line by Blomqvist, whose pulled-back centre was struck home by Magnus Erlingmark. All hope seemed lost for United when Gary Neville, replacing May, slipped as Blomqvist went by, leaving Pallister little alternative but to up-end him. As Pontus Kamark struck the penalty home it was as if United had stepped in front of the firing squad.

After Blomqvist was floored in the centre of the field Ince argued in language so fierce that Italian referee Alfredo Trentalange reached immediately for his red card. It was the final indignity for United.

Ferguson said: "My feeling is one of terrible disappointment without taking anything away from Gothenburg. I hope they go on to do well in the competition."

Not this time...
Thomas Ravelli foils
Andrei Kanchelskis.

November 26

If we had wanted to see a pack of Dobermans squabbling over a lump of raw meat we could have gone to Battersea Dogs Home rather than the re-modelled Highbury Stadium.

The managers tumbled out those familiar football war cries about character and commitment. More honestly there was simply a fear of defeat about both teams.

After two successive Premiership defeats Arsenal closed ranks, and did what they do better than any side in the country: squeezing the game.

United, shell-shocked in Sweden, travel-weary and ravaged by injuries, were unable to discover an antidote and in their frustration they lost their discipline, Mark Hughes suffering the disgrace of a red card.

This was an ill-tempered, vindictive contest that occasionally bordered on the violent, with an undertone of frenzy pouring from the packed terraces. It is four years since the players of these two proud clubs engaged in a shocking free-for-all at Old Trafford, squabbling like alley cats and scarring the game.

Some of the protagonists from that brawl are still around and perhaps it was that residual bad feeling which inflamed this game, with a little help from referee Kelvin Morton.

Arsenal boss George Graham spoke of what he felt was at stake. "It was more like a cup tie than a league game," he suggested. "When you have two sides who have dominated the last four years in terms of winning trophies, you are going to get a certain amount of the physical side. There was probably an over-commitment but I wish we had that every week."

Into this cauldron stepped referee Morton, cautioning young Keith Gillespie for a challenge while the fans were still settling in their seats for comfort.

That angered Alex Ferguson. "He booked him after just 23 seconds, yet he knows full well he is a young kid and a winger at that. You could hardly call the lad a tackler." Certainly Gillespie's careless lunge at Lee Dixon was far less sinister than some of the tackles that flew in later in the first half.

ARSENAL 0

MANCHESTER UNITED 0
(Half-time score : 0-0)

Arsenal: Seaman, Dixon, Bould, Adams, Winterburn, Morrow, Jensen (Keown 68), McGoldrick, Carter (Dickov 45), Wright, Smith.
United: Walsh, May, Neville, Pallister, Irwin, Kanchelskis (Butt 56), Ince, McClair, Gillespie (Davies 73), Cantona, Hughes.
Sub: Pilkington
Referee: K Morton (Bury St Edmunds).
Attendance: 38,301

Too often spectators were obliged to turn their heads sideways and wince, like you do when two cars are about to collide. Eddie McGoldrick and Hughes were both shown yellow cards but the really strong stuff was coming from Paul Ince, in one of his kamikaze moods, and his principal target John Jensen.

Meanwhile Eric Cantona was waving his arms about as if he were conducting the Philharmonic into the climax of the 1812 Overture. Just to spice up the dish Graham brought along his own Highland terrier to do a bit of snapping in the second half: young Paul Dickov, a little Scot with a lot of talent and a strong line in torment.

Ince tried to soften him up, too, before launching into a challenge with Jensen that put the Dane out of the game. Hughes completed his own personal indignity with a foul on Stephen Morrow. He walked even as Morton reached for the card.

In between the spite there was some football played and David Seaman had to tip the ball over the bar from Denis Irwin following one of Cantona's deft touches. Ian Wright responded with his own reminder of what the game should have been about and found Gary Walsh in similar resilient mood. They were isolated blooms in a crown of thorns.

Ferguson and Graham conspired to face the Press together afterwards, perhaps feeling they might share the embarrassment. Both are men of considerable substance and stature, sons of Glasgow who have come south to bring achievement to their clubs, the two longest-serving managers in the Premiership. And perhaps therein lay the problem.

Between them they have collected four league titles in the last six seasons. Both have also won the European Cup Winners' Cup, FA Cup and the League Cup. In the last two years, though, Arsenal have slipped in the Premiership, so there was more than the North-South divide resting on the fixture.

As Ferguson said: "Arsenal have their pride. They have had a bad week and so have we. It was head to head."

Perhaps someone should have banged their heads together and reminded them that after the events of the last week the last thing English football wanted was two of its most revered clubs behaving so badly.

League Table After Match

	P	W	D	L	F	A	Pts
Blackburn	16	11	3	2	35	13	36
Man Utd	16	11	2	3	31	10	35
Newcastle	16	10	4	2	34	17	34
Liverpool	16	9	3	4	33	17	30
Nottm Forest	16	8	4	4	25	16	28
Leeds	16	8	3	5	24	19	27
Man City	16	7	4	5	27	25	25
Chelsea	16	7	3	6	25	20	24
Norwich	16	6	6	4	15	14	24
Coventry	16	6	4	6	19	25	22
Southampton	16	5	6	5	23	26	21
Arsenal	16	5	5	6	18	16	20
C Palace	16	5	5	6	15	18	20
Tottenham	16	5	4	7	25	31	19
Sheff Wed	16	4	6	6	17	23	18
Wimbledon	16	5	3	8	17	28	18
West Ham	16	5	2	9	9	17	17
QPR	16	4	4	8	23	31	16
Aston Villa	16	3	5	8	20	28	14
Everton	16	3	5	8	12	24	14
Leicester	16	4	3	10	17	29	12
Ipswich	16	3	2	11	15	31	11

December 3

When Paul Ince's East-Ender voice bellows for his manager to make a substitution you realise the Old Trafford Soap Opera will contain some intriguing plot twists before its season ends.

Even in United's side of mega-stars not many players shout instructions across the ground to Alex Ferguson. Eric Cantona grunts. Mark Hughes growls. Only Ince barks and here he demanded that Ferguson got Andrei Kanchelskis, struggling with a stomach strain, off the pitch.

Such authority is not earned easily. But Ferguson is happy to see the one-time Cockney street fighter mark out his territory. Ince, who was battling against a shoulder knock, has Bryan Robson's knack of digging deeper as the pain mounts. "As the skipper I had to take responsibility," he said. "It was a case of gritting teeth and getting on with it. In the second half we lost our shape completely. It was important for me to get the other lads working. There were kids out there in our side. My job is to lift them and to sense the danger. Bryan Robson was always good at that. He spotted trouble before it happened. I like to do the same."

Cantona was United's mesmerist and scorer of the 36th-minute goal which kept them within a point of Blackburn. But Norwich boss John Deehan insisted it was Ince's drive and unquenchable spirit which denied his side a point.

Norwich, with their passing skills, went as close as any in the Premiership this season to knocking a hole in Fortress Old Trafford. No one has scored there in the league since Graeme Sharp hit Oldham's second in their 3-2 defeat last Easter Monday, 12 games ago.

Returning to their own backyard after the battles of Gothenburg and Highbury, United needed to remind us how they still intend to be the pick of the Premiership pack. Cantona and Ince certainly did their bit. So did the impressive Brian McClair, and it was his cross that Cantona converted nine minutes before half-time.

The Frenchman was in sublime form and would surely have won a penalty late on if he had gone down when John Polston nicked his foot. But he stumbled through off balance instead and the chance was gone.

MANCHESTER UNITED 1
NORWICH 0
(Half-time score : 1-0)

United: Walsh, Neville, Irwin, May, Kanchelskis (Butt 68), Pallister, Cantona, Ince, McClair, Hughes, Davies (Gillespie 56).
Sub: Pilkington.
Norwich: Gunn, Bowen, Newman (Cureton 63), Crook, Newsome, Bradshaw, Sutch, Ullathorne, Robins, Polston, Goss.
Scorer: Cantona 36.
Referee: T Holbrook (Walsall).
Attendance: 43,789

League Table After Match

	P	W	D	L	F	A	Pts
Blackburn	17	12	3	2	38	13	39
Man Utd	17	12	2	3	32	10	38
Newcastle	17	10	4	3	36	21	34
Liverpool	17	9	4	4	34	18	31
Nottm Forest	17	8	5	4	27	18	29
Man City	17	8	5	4	29	26	28
Chelsea	17	8	3	6	26	20	27
Leeds	16	8	3	5	24	19	27
Norwich	17	6	6	5	15	15	24
Coventry	17	6	5	6	20	27	23
Tottenham	17	6	4	7	29	33	22
Arsenal	17	5	6	6	20	18	21
Southampton	17	5	6	6	23	27	21
Sheff Wed	17	5	6	6	18	23	21
C Palace	17	5	5	7	15	19	20
QPR	17	5	4	8	25	32	19
Wimbledon	17	5	3	9	17	31	18
West Ham	17	5	2	10	10	19	17
Aston Villa	17	3	6	8	21	29	15
Everton	16	3	5	8	12	24	14
Leicester	17	3	4	10	18	30	13
Ipswich	17	3	2	12	16	33	11

By then Mark Robins, the lad who loved and lost a United career, reckoned he should have picked out an equaliser. Robins, the footballing son of an Oldham police inspector, was frustrated by a marginal offside decision. He was also aggrieved when young Gary Neville denied him a clear chance of a goal, earning a booking for snatching at Robins' arm on the edge of the box.

Robins, though, agreed readily that the man who shut down the space available to Deehan's crisp passing outfit was Ince. "He was everywhere, different class, brilliant," said Robins. "I think he's the best in the country."

With Ian Crook sitting in front of their back four and Jeremy Goss his normal mobile self, Norwich could still have grabbed a point in the last half-hour.

Eric Cantona fires in his goal.

But Gary Walsh handled everything with Peter Schmeichel's panache and, like 11 Premiership sides before them, Norwich left Old Trafford goalless.

December 7

Manchester United's European Cup season is a thing of the past but the future looks full of glittering potential for the English champions. The consolation in their exit from Europe's most prestigious club competition came from the teenage talent that manager Alex Ferguson paraded at Old Trafford last night. Four young players strutted their stuff with a swagger and sway that eased the pain of United's going.

Gary Neville, David Beckham, Nicky Butt and Simon Davies might not yet carry the same presence as Eric Cantona, Ryan Giggs, Andrei Kanchelskis and Lee Sharpe. Yet out of the depression of another abortive European campaign they offered a laser of light.

It had always seemed unlikely that United would advance to the quarter-finals when Barcelona needed only a draw against Gothenburg in the Nou Camp. And sure enough the miracle never happened.

As the goals flowed against the Turks we all knew it was 1,000 miles away in Barcelona that the significant action was unfolding as Gothenburg and Barcelona ended 1-1.

United went into their final Champions' League match ravaged by injury and suspensions to Paul Ince and Mark Hughes. But their proud record of 55 unbeaten European home ties over 38 years never seemed under threat.

Davies, from the up-and-under territory of St Helens, must have felt a shiver as he pulled Ryan Giggs' No 11 shirt over his head. Yet he set stout hearts fluttering with a goal in the third minute that put United on route for this crushing victory.

The pass for that goal was supplied by 19-year-old Neville, the full-back preferred to the more experienced David May, a decision fully justified by his mature, exhilarating performance, underlined by his willingness to get forward.

Butt has already made his European mark and continues to suggest he has the talent to stand comparison with Ince. Yet the pick of the choirboy quartet was Beckham, a player of courage and confidence. It was clear Eric Cantona loved having these kids around him and he went about his work like a cockerel showing a nest of chicks the way to use the pen.

MANCHESTER UNITED 4

GALATASARAY 0

(Half-time score : 2-0)

United: Walsh, Neville, Irwin, Bruce, Keane, Pallister, Cantona, Butt, McClair, Beckham, Davies. Booked: Cantona, Davies.
Galatasaray: Stauche, Ergun, Sedat, Mert, Tugay (Yusuf 62), Arif, Hamza (Ugar 45), Hakan, Suat, Kubilay, Bulent.
Scorers: Davies 2, Beckham 37, Keane 48, Bulent 87 og.
Referee: R Wojcik (Poland).
Attendance: 39,220

There is no refinement about the boys from Istanbul but their spitting and snarling never intimidated the youngsters. United's defence, who have experienced some torrid nights in this campaign, found they had little to fear from a Turkish side who lacked appetite once the first goal flashed in.

It was supplied by Neville from the right, a lovely deep centre that dipped over the head of the tireless Brian McClair and on to the chest of former youth skipper Davies. He let it bounce and then strode forward to drive his shot left-footed into the far corner.

Cantona had his statutory moment of madness, a lunge at Korkmaz that had Polish referee Ryszard Wojcik reaching for the yellow card that would have put Cantona out of the quarter-finals had United made it.

When Bulent's tackle on McClair in the 38th minute sent the ball spinning free Beckham hardly broke stride as he arrowed the ball inside the far post.

Two minutes into the second half Roy Keane collected Cantona's cross, flicked on by Beckham, and side-stepped two tackles before stroking the ball into the corner. Bulent added the final act of capitulation, slicing Cantona's cross into his own net in the dying moments.

December 10

The kid with the urchin's face looked shy as he offered a birthday card for Manchester United's senior players to sign when they arrived in their sleek cars at the club's training ground last August.

He might have been another of the wide-eyed day-dreamers who flock to The Cliff before a new season hoping for a smile and a pat on the head from their idols.

Paul Scholes received plenty of pats on the head from those same first-team players yesterday as he guaranteed their win bonus at QPR with a couple of glorious goals.

He might still have to know his place in the dressing room but when Scholes gets out on a pitch he is very much a man among equals, posing an interesting question for boss Alex Ferguson. With United free of Europe and its foreign rule, need he persevere with his quest to unburden his employers of around £5 million for an English centre-forward?

Les Ferdinand, one of Fergie's potential targets, paraded impressive credentials in this stirring contest, scoring one goal that prompted a quick intake of breath and another that spoke for his outstanding athleticism. Yet in a classic "anything you can do..." response 20-year-old Scholes headed a couple of his own and made another with the deftest of touches.

Ray Wilkins, who works with the England Under-21 side, may see Salford-born Scholes not only as a candidate for international football but also as the man to stave off possible Fergie overtures for Ferdy.

Coming as an encore to the performance of Fergie's Four in Europe in midweek, Scholes effort at Loftus Road prompted Wilkins to say: "United have as good a crop of young players as I have seen. It appears they had a very impressive youth team in the Ryan Giggs era because they are all of a similar age. Alex has used them magnificently well and they all know their function in the side."

He added: "Scholes' movement off the ball was exceptional. His lay-off for the goal Roy Keane scored was quite wonderful. He sees things early and for a little chap he's a good target.

"Even though United have players out injured, the people they can bring in are of a very high standard. It goes to show the depth they

---

QPR **2**

MANCHESTER UNITED **3**

(Half-time score : 1-2)

QPR: Dykstra, Maddix, Wilson, Bardsley, McDonald, Hodge, Barker, Impey, Ferdinand, Gallen, Sinclair.
United: Walsh, Neville (Gillespie 77), Irwin, Bruce, Keane, Pallister, Ince, Kanchelskis, McClair, Scholes, Davies (Butt 67).
Sub: Pilkington.
Scorers: (QPR): Ferdinand 23, 64; (United): Scholes 34, 47, Keane 44.
Referee: G Poll (Tilehurst).
Attendance: 18,948

have that the young guys who come in are very composed. They know how to play. They know their function. That is what makes them the best outfit in the Premiership."

It was generous praise from a gracious man who will make the most of his restricted resources at Rangers.

And if United had Scholes, so Wilkins had his own young gem in Kevin Gallen, Ferdinand's teenage partner, a tall boy with a good touch and an ability to hold the ball up in the manner of Mark Hughes.

"He's an old head on young shoulders," said Wilkins. "If he maintains his progress we may see a very good player. He's a confident lad with a belief in his own ability. That was a big stage for him today, playing against a terrific outfit.

"He is strong. I think Hughes is the best there is and, though Gallen's obviously still raw, he is very much like him in many aspects. He has a good physique and is prepared to work hard for the team."

United have still to reach the peak they attained last season and have not yet had an injury-free run. But that has served only to expose the rich seam beneath the lush surface.

Wilkins said: "A lot of clubs buy their way to success but you only have to look at Alex and what he is trying to do to see he has a lot of talented guys coming through who are home grown.

"They must have worked hard through their youth system to get that going. It can be tough on youngsters because there is always the threat of somebody being bought in. However, you can bet your bottom dollar that, if Alex Ferguson is prepared to play a lot of these chaps, he feels has no need to buy people and that must give the youngsters enormous confidence to go out and play."

Scholes had that confidence and in four months he has gone from the kid asking for autographs to the one signing them.

League Table After Match

	P	W	D	L	F	A	Pts
Blackburn	18	13	3	2	41	15	42
Man Utd	18	13	2	3	35	12	41
Newcastle	18	11	4	3	39	22	37
Nottm Forest	18	9	5	4	31	19	32
Liverpool	17	9	4	4	34	18	31
Man City	17	8	4	5	29	26	28
Leeds	18	8	4	6	26	24	28
Chelsea	18	8	3	7	26	23	27
Norwich	18	7	6	5	18	15	27
Tottenham	18	7	4	7	32	34	25
Coventry	18	6	5	7	20	29	23
Arsenal	17	5	6	6	20	18	21
Southampton	18	5	6	7	25	30	21
Sheff Wed	18	5	6	7	19	26	21
Wimbledon	18	6	3	9	19	31	21
C Palace	17	5	5	7	15	19	20
QPR	18	5	4	9	27	35	19
Everton	18	4	6	8	15	24	18
West Ham	18	5	3	10	12	21	18
Aston Villa	18	3	7	8	21	29	16
Leicester	18	3	4	11	19	33	13
Ipswich	18	3	2	13	17	37	11

December 17

Paul Ince charged Stuart Pearce – man-of-the-match by a huge margin – with making a racist remark after a bad-mouth scuffle. And manager Alex Ferguson, weighing in with the racist charge, also threw in a time-wasting accusation against Frank Clark's revived title contenders.

But the truth was that United's first home Premiership defeat since April, and the concession of their first goals on their own ground in league action in that time, deserves a more representative postscript.

Forest simply did more things right on the day. They also had Stan Collymore as well as Pearce.

Ince said: "A remark was made out there and it upset me."

What Pearce said, no doubt, would not have passed muster at a civilised gathering. But then, in a game of this passion, and under this pressure, the normal rules of politeness, indeed decency, have a tendency to fly through the window. This is not to be approved but it would be wearisome to recount the number of times black, Irish, Welsh, Scottish and these days Romanian players have had their origins, not to mention their parentage, abused in the heat of the action.

Racism, of course, is to be despised in all its forms and in all circumstances. But you had to believe this was a case of selective outrage.

In the end Ince should have been grateful that referee Keith Burge did not add his name to a lengthening list of players when he charged 30 yards after Bryan Roy to grapple and lay down his version of the law. Roy was booked for a foul but then he might have pleaded retaliation for an unpunished earlier foul on him by Ince.

Six Forest players – Steve Stone, Roy, Des Lyttle, Pearce, Ian Woan and Steve Chettle – were booked against United's Roy Keane and Ryan Giggs. That reflected the flow of the game in which United did most of the attacking and Forest defended with sustained combativeness and no little brilliance. Time wasting? It would have been surprising in the circumstances had there not been. But referee Burge warned Forest. . . and they took their chances with his timepiece.

Forest were worth their win because more of their players produced the kind of performances demanded in this kind of setting, and with these stakes involved. Pearce was all-consuming in his ambition and his control.

MANCHESTER UNITED 1

NOTTINGHAM FOREST 2

(Half-time score : 0-1)

United: Walsh, Keane, Irwin, Bruce, Kanchelskis (Neville 87), Pallister, Cantona, Ince, McClair, Hughes, Giggs (Butt 75).
Sub: Pilkington.
Forest: Crossley, Lyttle, Pearce, Haaland, Chettle, Phillips, Roy (Bohinen 85), Gemmill, Woan, Collymore, Stone.
Scorers: (United): Cantona 68; (Forest): Collymore 35, Pearce 62.
Referee: K Burge (Tonypandy).
Attendance: 43,744

For England boss Terry Venables the video of this game might serve not as a cry from the dark by the former national team skipper but a reminder that in the nitty-gritty of top-level competition the Forest man probably still has a sharp edge on the exuberant young Graeme Le Saux.

While Stone and Chettle produced performances of superb commitment, the other decisive dimension belonged to Collymore. Despite a woeful lack of support from the quick but mostly inconsequential Roy, Collymore brought neurosis to Steve Bruce and Gary Pallister. Bruce was undermined in the first minutes when Collymore ate up the ground to rob the United skipper and was then denied a shattering early goal only by the brilliant intervention of Ince.

Collymore swept Forest into the lead with the sweetest of shots as Pallister shaped to make a tackle. It was all too quick, too powerful for England's resident central defender.

Collymore's manager denied there had been approaches from United for the striker and insisted he would do all he could to keep the big man at the City Ground. But Clark is a practical man and he agreed that every club has its price. According to market forces, a reasonable one for Collymore right now is £6-7 million.

Yes, said Collymore, he did rate his chances of bursting into the England strikers' club. "It was a pity the goals had dried up a bit before the England B team were selected," he said. "But they're coming again now and I'm confident I can play at the highest level. It's just a case of doing my job and proving my point."

That may not be just to Venables. Ferguson's reluctance to grant Mark Hughes an extended contract is the clearest admission that he is looking for new, younger and English finishing power. He need look no further than Collymore.

Clark conceded that Alan Shearer is demonstrably England's best striker. But then who? Collymore's power and skill off both feet, his deceptive speed, his "bottle" in the close situations, make him the dream candidate.

His goal set the tone of the afternoon, building uncertainty into a United effort which could not be transformed by Cantona's goal from a corner by Giggs. The United winger was withdrawn mysteriously just as he seemed to be making tentative steps away from his recent nightmare.

Forest had moved further ahead earlier in the second half when, appropriately, Pearce drove in off Bruce from a corner. United had protested about the time Forest took to produce the corner-kick. They would have been better off getting their marking right.

League Table After Match

	P	W	D	L	F	A	Pts
Blackburn	19	13	4	2	41	15	43
Man Utd	19	13	2	4	36	14	41
Newcastle	19	11	5	3	39	22	38
Nottm Forest	19	10	5	4	33	20	35
Liverpool	18	9	5	4	34	18	32
Leeds	19	9	4	6	29	25	31
Norwich	19	8	6	5	19	15	30
Man City	19	8	4	7	30	31	28
Chelsea	18	8	3	7	26	23	27
Tottenham	19	7	5	7	32	34	26
Arsenal	19	6	6	7	23	22	24
Coventry	19	6	6	7	20	29	24
QPR	19	6	4	9	29	35	22
Wimbledon	19	6	4	9	21	33	22
Southampton	18	5	6	7	25	30	21
C Palace	19	5	6	8	15	20	21
West Ham	19	6	3	10	15	21	21
Sheff Wed	19	5	6	8	19	28	21
Everton	19	4	7	8	15	24	19
Aston Villa	18	3	7	8	21	29	16
Leicester	19	3	5	11	19	33	14
Ipswich	19	3	3	13	19	39	12

Cantona scores United's only goal against Forest.

December 26

CHELSEA 2
MANCHESTER UNITED 3
(Half-time score : 0-1)

Chelsea: Kharine, Clarke, Sinclair, Spencer, Furlong, Peacock, Burley (Stein 54), Myers, Spackman, Hoddle (Newton 73), Johnsen.
United: Walsh, Irwin, Bruce, Pallister, Cantona, Ince (Neville 46), McClair, Hughes, Giggs, Keane, Butt (Kanchelskis 76).
Sub: Pilkington.
Scorers: (United): Hughes 21, Cantona 46 pen, McClair 78; (Chelsea): Spencer 58 pen, Newton 77
Referee: M Reed (Birmingham)
Attendance: 31,161

When it comes to capital gains Manchester United have emerged with lucrative profits this season. Their success at Chelsea yesterday was their third in London.

But the tax they put on their supporters can be a burden. In their High Noon showdown against the team that had the audacity to do the double over them last season, they surrendered a two-goal advantage before Brian McClair ensured they kept the pressure on Blackburn Rovers.

It was a fine match and manager Alex Ferguson had emotions mixed between satisfaction and relief at the end of it.

Chelsea taunted their visitors at Stamford Bridge by playing Montserrat Caballé and Freddie Mercury's rousing rendition of "Barcelona" over the tannoy, but the real harmony out on the pitch came from United. It flowed from Eric Cantona and Roy Keane, both singing from the same song sheet and with barely a note out of place.

Some of the passing from United in the first half was exquisite, a distinct advantage on this postage-stamp pitch which even Chelsea manager Glenn Hoddle complains about.

Chelsea might have counted themselves fortunate to be only a goal down at half-time because United had chances they might have been expected to finish more clinically. Yet a United penalty in the first move of the second half looked to have locked up the result.

United's players apparently thought so because they fell back into cruise mode, that infuriating casual approach which is a suicidal facet of their nature. A Gary Pallister push gave away a penalty and Chelsea were back in it.

Ferguson said: "It nearly turned out a disaster for us which I didn't envisage at 2-0. We relaxed and got careless. The passing in the first half was absolutely superb. We had kept good possession and had good penetration and played superbly. They got back with what looked a softish penalty and when they equalised I thought, "What a throwaway this is'."

The absence of Dennis Wise, so much the driving force for Cheslea, was always going to be a critical loss and Paul Ince took charge of a midfield where Ferguson added an extra player.

Super Red

Above Liverpool goalkeeper David James is powerless as Kanchelskis chips to score.

Right A delighted Kanchelskis after scoring against Gothenburg in the Champions League.

United Strike

Above Brian McClair shooting against Liverpool in September.

Right Paul Scholes after scoring in United's 2-1 victory over Port Vale in the Coca-Cola Cup.

Opposite page West Ham's Steve Potts becomes a human ladder only for Ince to see his shot go wide.

Happiness and Heartache

Right An elated Kanchelskis after scoring a hat-trick against Manchester City.

Below And another goal, this time against Crystal Palace.

Opposite page (top) You're off! Paul Ince gets the red card during United's Champions League match against Gothenburg

Opposite page (bottom) Ince injures his ankle blocking a shot from Arsenal's John Jensen.

Celebrations

Above and right Celebrations all round during United's 4-0 win over Galatasaray in the Champions League.

Opposite page (top) Ince dribbles past Chelsea's Glenn Hoddle …

Opposite page (bottom) … and McClair scores.

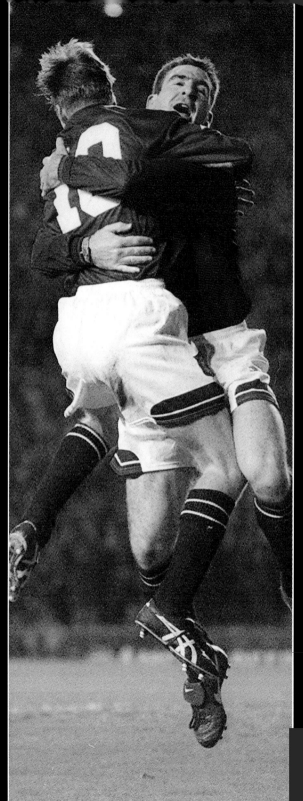

Goal!

Above Ooh, ah Cantona … praise from his team-mates after he scores against Coventry.

Right Newcastle's Paul Kitson gets past the United defence to score.

Opposite page (top) Scholes and Keane play piggy back after United's win against QPR …

Opposite page (bottom) Hughes and Giggs celebrate with Nicky Butt after his goal in the New Year's Eve game against Southampton.

The United All Stars

Above United's England players, Lee Sharpe, Andy Cole and Gary Pallister.

Right Cole and Cantona in training before the big clash with Blackburn Rovers.

Opposite page January 1995: Andy Cole becomes the latest member of Alex Ferguson's elite.

Communicate
and Contemplate

Left Crowd-pleasing Cantona.
Below Alex Ferguson and Brian Kidd getting the point across during United's FA Cup win over Wrexham.

"I sacrificed a winger," he said, "partly to compensate for the narrowness of the pitch and partly because of the diamond formation Chelsea play which troubled us last season with Gavin Peacock making his runs off the two strikers."

This looked a flawed gem in the first half and Ince was scratching away at it successfully until he pulled a hamstring stretching into a challenge with Craig Burley in the 42nd minute.

By then United had quite properly taken the lead from a goal of stunning simplicity. McClair's ball down the line was picked up by the accelerating Ryan Giggs. Over came the cross from the left, Cantona distracted the defence and, as the ball dipped over him, Mark Hughes came in from behind like a battering ram to score.

Worse followed for Chelsea seconds after half-time as the most delicate of flicks from Cantona saw Keane charging into the penalty area. Frank Sinclair sent the Irishman flying full-length and referee Mike Reed had no alternative to giving the penalty.

Visions of last season's FA Cup final, when he gave away a penalty must have flashed through Sinclair's mind. Cantona stroked the ball home from the spot, as he did twice at Wembley.

Less certain was Chelsea's penalty after 58 minutes because, although Pallister clearly nudged Chelsea substitute Mark Stein in the back, it looked outside the area. John Spencer thumped home the kick and suddenly the decibel count was up. It rose again as the industrious Paul Furlong swung in a cross for Eddie Newton to head the equaliser.

Chelsea then committed the sin of losing their concentration and within a minute Keane had run at their defence, Cantona had helped the ball on and McClair had stroked it home.

Hughes celebrates his goal with Roy Keane and Nicky Butt.

December 28

MANCHESTER UNITED 1
LEICESTER 1
(Half-time score : 0-0)

United: Walsh, Neville, Irwin, Bruce, Kanchelskis, Pallister, Cantona, Keane, McClair, Hughes (Scholes 69), Giggs.
Subs: May, Pilkington.
Leicester: Poole, Grayson, Whitlow, Willis, Hill, Agnew, Thompson, Oldfield (Lowe 68), Roberts, Draper, Philpott (Blake 73).
Scorers: (United): Kanchelskis 61; (Leicester): Whitlow 65.
Referee: D Gallagher (Banbury).
Attendance: 43,789

Mark McGhee vowed he would not play the apprentice to Old Trafford sorcerer Alex Ferguson and emerged with the best result of his embryonic managerial career.

Blackburn's Kenny Dalglish, recuperating from an appendix operation, could only have been deeply grateful. With Rovers' match against Leeds washed out, a United victory would have put them back on top of the table.

It did not happen because in three games McGhee has revolutionised floundering Filbert Street. Ferguson, annoyed at seeing five points slip away in the last two home games, admitted: "We got no more than we deserved. We just didn't create enough chances and there was not enough quality in our play. It was poor, really. We had fantastic pressure in the second half but did not get quality crosses in. That stopped us making the chances to hurt them."

McGhee and Ferguson have been linked since McGhee became Fergie's first signing of Aberdeen's golden era 15 years ago. And not even a stormy relationship that saw Ferguson, in his own words, "hand out more brickbats than bouquets" disturbed the mutual respect. The bond encouraged Ferguson personally to recommend McGhee for the manager's jobs at Reading and Leicester.

McGhee, though, was clearly not prepared to treat this Premiership affair as a tutorial. After overseeing a draw against Blackburn and defeat by Liverpool – both at Filbert Street – the new Leicester boss ordered his side to attack every inch of a sodden Old Trafford.

Even so, Ryan Giggs had an early chance to spoil Leicester's plans as he chased on to a pass from Gary Pallister. But the Welsh flier went a yard too far, and as the angle closed, could only fire his left-footer into the side-netting.

In a second half in which Giggs showed increasing evidence that he is recovering from the slump in form which had blighted his season it was the man on the opposite flank who broke the Leicester blockade. On the hour Andrei Kanchelskis grabbed the ball as Mark Hughes robbed defender Colin Hill, homed in from the left and hammered a missile beyond Kevin Poole.

It was the Ukrainian's 12th goal of the season but within five minutes Leicester had bounced back. Lee Philpott's high corner was lost by Walsh and defender Mike Whitlow was on hand to bundle in the equaliser.

Whitlow was inadvertently responsible for Hughes being taken out of the action shortly afterwards. Hughes, already booked for a foul, was lucky to escape a second card as he barged into the full-back. Ferguson decided discretion was needed before the striker got his marching orders and brought Paul Scholes on for the final 20 minutes.

Later McGhee backed Ferguson to lift the title next spring. He said: "I didn't expect to get beaten but United will still be champions. I played for Alex for five years at Aberdeen. To win things you need the best players and that's what he has got here."

Leicester goal hero Whitlow said: "Gary Neville appeared to get in Walsh's way for my goal. I just put my toe in and it was over the line. I was a big United fan when I played for Witton Albion and my old mates will be giving me a lot of stick tonight."

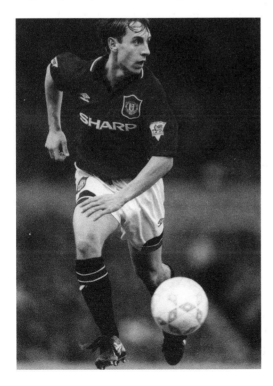

Gary Neville on the defensive.

League Table After Match

	P	W	D	L	F	A	Pts
Blackburn	20	14	4	2	44	16	46
Man Utd	21	14	3	4	40	17	45
Liverpool	21	11	6	4	38	19	39
Newcastle	20	11	6	3	39	22	39
Nottm Forrest	21	11	6	4	34	20	39
Leeds	20	9	5	6	29	25	32
Norwich	21	8	6	7	19	18	30
Tottenham	21	8	6	7	34	34	30
Arsenal	21	7	7	7	25	22	28
Chelsea	21	8	4	9	28	29	28
Man City	21	8	4	9	31	36	28
Wimbledon	21	8	4	9	25	35	28
Sheff Wed	21	7	6	8	28	30	27
Southampton	21	6	7	8	31	36	25
Coventry	21	6	7	8	21	34	25
QPR	21	6	6	9	31	37	24
C Palace	21	5	8	8	15	20	23
West Ham	21	6	4	11	16	23	22
Aston Villa	21	4	8	9	25	31	20
Everton	20	4	7	9	16	28	19
Leicester	21	3	6	12	21	36	15
Ipswich	21	3	4	14	20	42	13

December 31

SOUTHAMPTON 2

MANCHESTER UNITED 2

(Half-time score : 1-0)

Southampton: Grobbelaar, Kenna, Benali, Magilton, Monkou, Le Tissier, Dowie, Hughes, Widdrington, Ekelund (Heaney 66), Dodd.
United: Walsh, Bruce, Pallister, Cantona, McClair (Gillespie 79), Hughes, Giggs, May, Keane, Butt, Neville.
Subs: Scholes, Pilkington.
Scorers: (Southampton): Magilton 44, Hughes 74; (United): Butt 51, Pallister 78.
Referee: M Bodenham (Cornwall).
Attendance: 15,204

Having scaled the Premiership mountain twice, Manchester United clearly feel that this season they should take a more circuitous climb to the summit.

What befell them at The Dell might be nothing more menacing than a snowstorm but they must beware an avalanche of lost points. United are 14 adrift of the position they held this time last season.

"Winning the league the first time gave us great confidence and then last year we got off to such a great start and played some brilliant football right through to spring," Alex Ferguson said. "This year we have been caught between the domestic and the Champions' leagues and we have had more injuries, so it has been difficult to pick the team at times."

With Blackburn above them and Liverpool advancing threateningly from base camp, the race for the championship may be more open than United thought.

Steve Bruce warned: "I think there could be four or five teams in it, especially if one of them puts together a strong nine – or 10-match run. We shall be doing our utmost in the next few matches to haul back the three points Blackburn have on us at the moment."

Southampton manager Alan Ball, who has scaled a few heights himself as a player, said: "United and Blackburn are both very good sides but I think I would put my money on United. They have more strength in depth and Old Trafford is a more intimidating place for opponents than Ewood Park.

"You are never comfortable because they have so many good players in their side; players who like to go forward and who can win games. I am certainly not going to write off Blackburn. But I feel that, if United have to put their foot on the gas, they can."

United had to claw their way back twice after losing their footing at The Dell where, despite having Paul Ince and Andrei Kanchelskis as significant absentees, their commitment to attack was unwavering.

Nicky Butt's growing maturity was confirmed with a first Premiership goal and an all-round performance which was a delightful cameo in a fine, flowing game.

Ball added: "One of United's secrets is they don't ask good players to play safety-first football. It is what I am trying to instill into my young team, to keep playing good, bright football and be involved in entertaining matches every week. You have to be satisfied to get something against the best.

"I said to my lads that if they went out in awe they would get rolled over. I told them just to get out and have a go and earn United's respect."

Ball's comments underlined the fact that teams raise their standard against United, so any relaxation of their own standards is usually punished, as it was in this highly charged, competitive game.

"Southampton deserved to be in front at half-time because we were lax and second to too many balls," said Ferguson. "But we buckled down in the second half and showed a great deal more urgency.

"This was symptomatic of the type of game we are involved in away from home. It was a cup tie atmosphere and Southampton deserved their point."

It was a generous gesture from Fergie and, despite some bizarre refereeing decisions from Martin Bodenham, the United manager was in convivial mood after his New Year CBE.

"I am not getting involved in talking about the referee," he said. "I am a man of great repute now. In fact, I don't know why I am talking to you!"

He could joke because he knows United still have the summit in their sights and, with a game against Blackburn looming on January 21, they might be taking a stronger foothold.

League Table After Match

	P	W	D	L	F	A	Pts
Blackburn	21	15	4	2	45	16	49
Man Utd	22	14	4	4	42	19	46
Liverpool	22	12	6	4	40	19	42
Newcastle	21	11	6	4	40	24	39
Nottm Forrest	22	11	6	5	35	23	39
Tottenham	22	9	6	7	38	34	33
Norwich	22	9	6	7	21	19	33
Leeds	21	9	5	7	29	27	32
Sheff Wed	22	8	6	8	29	30	30
Chelsea	22	8	5	9	29	30	29
Man City	22	8	5	9	33	38	29
Wimbledon	22	8	5	9	26	36	29
Arsenal	22	7	7	8	26	25	28
QPR	22	7	6	9	34	38	27
Southampton	22	6	8	8	33	38	26
West Ham	22	7	4	11	19	24	25
Coventry	22	6	7	9	21	38	25
C Palace	22	5	8	9	15	21	23
Everton	21	5	7	9	20	29	22
Aston Villa	22	4	9	9	27	33	21
Leicester	22	3	6	13	21	37	15
Ipswich	22	3	4	15	21	46	13

January 3

MANCHESTER UNITED 2
COVENTRY 0
(Half-time score : 1-0)

United: Walsh, Neville, Irwin, Bruce, Gillespie, Pallister, Cantona, Keane (McClair 64), Scholes, Butt, Giggs.
Subs: May, Pilkington.
Coventry: Ogrizovic, Pickering, Morgan, Williams, Marsh, Pressley, Flynn (Jones 82), Wegerle (Darby 53), Dublin, Jenkinson, Cook.
Scorers: Scholes 29, Cantona 49 pen.
Referee: G Willard (Worthing).
Attendance: 43,130

Alex Ferguson hailed Old Trafford rookie Paul Scholes as a kid with the Denis Law style as Manchester United moved within three points of Premiership leaders Blackburn.

At 5ft 6in and with a close crop of carrot-coloured hair, Scholes does not measure up physically to Eric Cantona or Mark Hughes. But when the chance came to show England's club biggest audience he can do the business at the highest level, the 20-year-old Salford boy took it.

With Hughes left out by manager Alex Ferguson, Scholes found himself operating alongside the imperious figure of Cantona. And two crucial interventions by this latest member of Fergie's famous finishing school turned the match away from a desperate Coventry.

City manager Phil Neal has had a macabre Christmas and could have done without the sight of young Scholes turning like a top to whip in United's opener in the first half. Scholes, who scored twice on his last senior outing when Hughes was suspended, gave Cantona a chance to wrap it up neatly from the penalty spot after the break when he was up-ended by Coventry defender Steven Pressley.

Pressley was sent off in the process and Coventry, with 10 men for the last 40 minutes, had no chance of stopping United moving within three points of Premiership leaders Blackburn.

Neal's side had been stricken by a starvation Christmas diet of one point from three games to go alongside a dreadful casualty list. Yet with Dion Dublin back at Old Trafford and with a point to prove, the visitors might have taken a 12th-minute lead.

Dublin, the tall, elegant attacker, left Old Trafford in September for £2 million after an injury-plagued two-year spell. His Highfield Road career began with 10 goals in 13 outings before injury waylaid him again for six games.

But when the new £450,000 midfielder Mike Marsh sent a free-kick into the United box Dublin's glanced back-header was met by the upright arm of Gary Pallister. It looked a hazardous gesture by the England centre-back but referee Gary Willard decided contact was unintentional.

Coventry's early ambition was in disarray on the half-hour as Keith

Gillespie whipped over a low cross. Nicky Butt back-heeled the ball and keeper Steve Ogrizovic could only palm it into the path of Scholes, who whirled round and potted his sixth goal in 13 games.

United operated without the fire of Andrei Kanchelskis on the right flank because the Ukrainian is booked to see a specialist over a persistent stomach strain this morning. But the exuberance of United's young stand-ins rolled them forward relentlessly and the game was over within four minutes of half-time.

Scholes robbed centre-back Pressley 25 yards out and, when the Coventry defender caught him in the box, referee Willard consulted his linesman before awarding the penalty. With Pressley already heading for an early bath, Cantona strolled up to knock a precise spot-kick inside Ogrizovic's right-hand post.

The dismissal knocked the stuffing out of Neal's faltering side and there were strident United claims for another penalty when Paul Williams brought down the flying Gillespie. Coventry substitute Julian Darby also diced with the fates when he tackled Cantona heavily in the box. With United substitute Brian McClair eagerly joining the assault, it could easily have been 4-0 by the final whistle.

Ferguson was lavish in his praise of Scholes. "The boy has certainly put himself in the frame for further matches," he said. "His run for the goal was brilliant. He started from the back post and came in to nick it. It was the sort of goal Denis Law used to get here for fun. A real poacher's effort."

The United boss also praised his three others fledglings – Gillespie, Butt and Gary Neville. "All young players make mistakes. These lads did so tonight but they always wanted to try things. That's what's called bottle and I was delighted with them."

League Table After Match

	P	W	D	L	F	A	Pts
Blackburn	22	16	4	2	49	18	52
Man Utd	23	15	4	4	44	19	49
Liverpool	23	13	6	4	44	19	45
Nottm Forest	23	12	6	5	36	23	42
Newcastle	22	11	7	4	40	24	40
Tottenham	23	10	6	7	39	34	36
Leeds	22	9	6	7	29	27	33
Norwich	23	9	6	8	21	23	33
Wimbledon	23	9	5	9	28	37	32
Sheff Wed	23	8	7	8	30	31	31
Man City	23	8	6	9	33	38	30
Chelsea	22	8	5	9	29	30	29
Arsenal	23	7	7	9	26	26	28
QPR	22	7	6	9	34	38	27
Southampton	23	6	9	8	34	39	27
West Ham	23	7	4	12	21	28	25
Coventry	23	6	7	10	21	40	25
C Palace	23	5	8	10	15	22	23
Aston Villa	23	4	10	9	27	33	22
Everton	22	5	7	10	21	31	22
Ipswich	23	4	4	15	25	47	16
Leicester	23	3	6	14	22	41	15

January 9

SHEFFIELD UNITED 0

MANCHESTER UNITED 2

(Half-time score : 0-0)

Sheff Wed: Kelly, Gage, Nilsen, Hartfield, Gayle, Whitehouse (Flo 86), Rogers, Veart, Blake, Hodges (Starbuck 76), Scott.
United: Schmeichel, Irwin, Bruce, Keane, Pallister, Cantona, Butt, McClair (Scholes 78), Hughes, Giggs, O'Kane (Sharpe 65).
Sub: Pilkington.
Scorers: Hughes 80, Cantona 82.
Referee: R Hart (Darlington).
Attendance: 22,322

Eric Cantona came through to seal United's FA Cup victory and earn a fourth-round FA Cup tie against Wrexham. He was accused of provoking Charlie Hartfield into the face slap that left the First Division side battling with 10 men from the 14th minute.

Hartfield insisted that Cantona had aimed a kick at his ankle in the incident that brought his dismissal by referee Robbie Hart. Hartfield admitted: "I just lost my head in the heat of the moment. I'm choked about what happened."

But Hartfield got no sympathy from manager Dave Bassett, "Charlie says he got a tap on the ankle and reacted. He knows he cost us the game. He says he was clumped. I don't care if it was Cantona or anyone else who did it, Charlie knows you can't take the law into your own hands on the pitch. He was stupid to get himself sent off because Manchester United are the last side in the world you want to face with 10 men. It's going to cost Charlie three matches plus a week's wages. He'll look back on this moment for the rest of his life. But overall I was pleased with my boys' performance. Manchester United must have thought it was bonus day. I wish one of their players had done that to us!"

Ferguson's team gradually made the extra man tell, wearing down Sheffield's resistance. A Hughes header in the 80th minute did the damage. And two minutes later Cantona added the most exquisite of postscripts.

However, United, flu-hit and forced to usher Schmeichel back before his bruised disc was ready, had a desperate start. The goalkeeper could only parry a Nathan Blake shot, and as the ball rolled across the line, young John O'Kane's attempt to clear hit Glyn Hodges and was flashing back towards the net before Schmeichel made a superb save. Aussie Carl Veart headed back a Paul Rogers cross into the path of the bustling Blake and Steve Bruce smashed into him. The penalty whistle but it never came but tempers were up.

Sure enough, when Rogers then felled Nicky Butt a bustling throng of players got involved, up came Cantona's foot, across came the slap from Hartfield and out of the window went Bassett's Cup ambitions.

United took control of the midfield, Roy Keane enjoying the freedom.

There was a brief but encouraging second-half appearance for Lee Sharpe after 10 weeks out with an ankle injury.

Twice Hughes met Ryan Giggs' crosses; the first forced the excellent Alan Kelly into a fine save, the second smashed against the upright.

Steve Bruce and Denis Irwin earned cautions for challenges on Veart, Bruce moving past the 35-point mark and into a two-match suspension.

It was one-way traffic in the second half. The driving young Butt had a lovely lob tipped over and put two other shots just off target. It was left to Hughes to show the clinical finish. Paul Scholes and Keane worked the opening and Giggs hit the cross which the Welshman headed home.

The relief was immeasurable and United began to toy with the shattered Sheffield players. Giggs again split them wide open with a ball to Cantona on the edge of the penalty area. The Frenchman looked up, saw Kelly coming off his line and gently lobbed him.

He stood there, then turned to the Sheffield fans who had been taunting him. You could almost hear the words of *The Wonder of You*.

Eric Cantona is attacked by Ryan Giggs after scoring for United.

January 15

NEWCASTLE 1
MANCHESTER UNITED 1
(Half-time score : 0-1)

Newcastle: Srnicek, Venison, Beresford, Peacock, Howey, Elliott, Fox, Lee, Kitson, Hottiger, Clark.
United: Schmeichel, Irwin, Bruce, Keane, Pallister, Cantona, Butt (May 45), McClair, Hughes (Scholes 15), Giggs, Sharpe.
Sub: Walsh.
Scorers: (Newcastle): Kitson 67; (United): Hughes 13.
Referee: S Lodge (Barnsley).
Attendance: 34,471

Mark Hughes' season was thought to be over as he was carried off with an injured knee. Alex Ferguson even feared his Welsh striker had damaged cruciate ligaments as he courageously scored United's goal.

In the event it was no worse than a deep gash for Hughes, a £2.5 million target for Everton following the arrival of £7 million Andy Cole at Old Trafford.

Hughes suffered the injury which needed 12 stitches, in a collision with Newcastle goalkeeper Pavel Srnicek, who came charging out of his goal feet first in a bid to block Hughes' 13th-minute strike.

Ferguson said: "Some goalkeepers come out with their hands, some come diving out like that, but Mark would never stop anyway. The chance was there for him to take."

In the circumstances the champions were relieved to get a point even though they are now trailing leaders Blackburn by five. Newcastle fans gave manager Kevin Keegan an amazingly supportive reception following the sale of Cole.

Newcastle were seriously pumped up for action and it was Cole's immediate replacement, £2.25 million marksman Paul Kitson, who hit the equaliser midway through the second half.

Keegan claimed the vote of confidence from his fans came as no surprise. "I don't expect anything else from these fans but it wasn't so much me they were getting behind as the team."

Ferguson was grateful for a point for, in addition to Hughes, Roy Keane suffered a hamstring problem and another booking lines him up for a two-match ban. Nicky Butt was replaced at half-time because of double vision and skipper Steve Bruce was succumbing to flu, forcing United to finish the game with three central defenders.

"We didn't deserve a point and were fortunate to come away with one," admitted Ferguson. It was fair comment because, if Keegan had firm backing from the stands, he also received Trojan effort from his team.

The loss of Hughes had a profound effect on the champions, their football becoming disjointed and fragile.

Yet United could barely have begun in more encouraging fashion.

Keane crossed from the right and Hughes slid the ball home as Cantona swayed out of the way like a matador evading a bull's horn. But in the instant Hughes made contact, Srnicek's boot caught him like a surgeon's scalpel.

Newcastle had two chances just before half-time, Steve Howey missing his kick from only 10 yards and Robert Lee driving another of Kitson's lay-offs skimming over the bar.

Keegan's side deserved some reward for their persistence and it came in the 67th minute as the probing Lee again got the ball into the Manchester area. This time Kitson got a lucky rebound off Gary Pallister and, as Peter Schmeichel came off his line, he struck the ball straight between his legs. It was a sweet goal for a man charged with the awful responsibility of replacing Cole.

There were three promising chances for United in the last seven minutes, Keane just failing to thread the ball through Srnicek's legs and Cantona wide with two shots he would expect to put away as a matter of habit.

League Table After Match

	P	W	D	L	F	A	Pts
Blackburn	23	17	4	2	52	18	55
Man Utd	24	15	5	4	45	20	50
Liverpool	24	13	6	5	44	20	45
Nottm Forest	24	12	6	6	36	26	42
Newcastle	23	11	8	4	41	25	41
Tottenham	24	11	6	7	41	35	39
Wimbledon	24	10	5	9	30	38	35
Leeds	23	9	7	7	29	27	34
Norwich	24	9	6	9	22	25	33
Sheff Wed	24	8	8	8	31	32	32
Man City	24	8	7	9	33	38	31
Chelsea	23	8	6	9	30	31	30
Arsenal	24	7	8	9	27	27	29
Southampton	24	6	10	8	34	39	28
QPR	23	7	6	10	35	40	27
C Palace	24	6	8	10	17	22	26
Coventry	24	6	8	10	21	40	26
Aston Villa	24	5	10	9	29	34	25
West Ham	24	7	4	13	22	30	25
Everton	23	5	8	10	22	32	23
Ipswich	24	5	4	15	26	47	19
Leicester	24	3	6	15	22	43	15

Mark Hughes slides into score for Manchester United.

January 22

MANCHESTER UNITED 1

BLACKBURN 0

(Half-time score : 0-0)

United: Schmeichel, Keane, Irwin, Bruce, Sharpe (Kanchelskis 76), Pallister, Cantona, Ince, McClair, Cole, Giggs.
Subs: May, Walsh.
Blackburn: Flowers, Berg, Wright, Sherwood, Hendry, Le Saux, Atkins (Pearce 89), Warhurst, Shearer, Sutton, Wilcox (Newell 89).
Scorer: Cantona 80.
Referee: P A Durkin (Portland).
Attendance: 43,742

They packed the Theatre of Dreams to see £7 million debutant Andy Cole top the bill, yet the standing ovation went to that great impresario Eric Cantona.

The Frenchman is not a performer to be upstaged and, when Cole fluffed his lines, Cantona stepped forward in the 80th minute to deliver his own eloquent soliloquy.

Just what effect this thoroughly deserved victory will have on the remainder of Manchester United's season is a matter for speculation but its importance cannot be understated. It claws them to within two points of Blackburn at the top of the Premiership and, with a game to come at Crystal Palace before Rovers play again, United could be top by mid-week.

We had expected to be thrilled by the tension and spectacle of the occasion and were not disappointed even if Cole's contribution proved to be tortuous rather than tumultuous.

It might all have been so different for Cole because the fates offered him the chance of a dream start to his United career. Just 90 seconds into the game Brian McClair's dipping ball into the area caught Paul Warhurst a yard too far forward and the ball bounced perfectly for Cole.

He chested it down and the goal loomed large but in the haste of the moment he sliced his shot wide. It was Faldo missing a 12-inch putt, Hick dropping a dolly catch or Agassi serving a double fault on match point.

In that moment Cole's confidence drained from him as from a bath tap turned on full and for the rest of this breathless match he was largely a peripheral figure.

His day will come, sooner rather than later, for there are few centre-halves in Europe at present more formidable to face than the ice-cool Colin Hendry.

Hendry and Henning Berg toiled heroically in the face of sweeping United attacks and must have felt as if they were facing a riptide.

It was all the more disappointing for them, then, that it was Berg who was dispossessed by Ryan Giggs for the revitalised Welsh sorcerer to cross the ball deep to the far post and curling towards the upright. There was little margin for error and Cantona needed none as he soared to head the ball in.

United were inspired throughout by Paul Ince, the most energetic man on the field despite his recent absence, exploring every space and tracking every Rovers move.

Ince and McClair won the battle for midfield ascendancy over Tim Sherwood and Mark Atkins in a competitive contest and the result was that United were in control of a frenzied first half.

It was reassuring for lovers of the Beautiful Game that Giggs was back swaying and weaving beyond opponents. Giggs saw Cole and McClair miss chances before missing one himself, driving at the advancing Tim Flowers when a delicate chip over the goalkeeper would have done the trick.

Cantona and Steve Bruce, cautioned in the first half, were joined by Alan Wright and Chris Sutton early in the second as Rovers announced their intention of stepping on the gas. Shearer drove a cross from Sutton wide of the near post and then delivered a wayward shot after Peter Schmeichel made his one mistake of the match with a poor throw-out.

Anxiety was growing among the 43,742 crowd when the persistent Giggs first lost the ball to Berg, then regained it before hitting a centre of real quality for Cantona to score.

Even then the excitement was not over. In the 90th minute Berg crossed from the right and Shearer climbing with Keane, won a header across the box which Sherwood headed in despite the attentions of Bruce and Schmeichel. There was a moment's disbelieving silence before it became clear that referee Paul Durkin had blown for a push by Shearer on Keane and the goal was ruled out.

Kenny Dalglish dubbed the decision a "disgrace". "That decision could be the difference between the title being won and lost," rapped Rovers' manager. "If there had been a foul on Keane by Shearer he would have reacted straight away. The fact is Keane misjudged it. I couldn't see anything wrong with the goal at all.

"I've spoken to the referee but the only explanation you get is that he gave it as he saw it. I suppose he has to defend his actions. They say

	P	W	D	L	F	A	Pts
Blackburn	24	17	4	3	52	19	55
Man Utd	25	16	5	4	46	20	53
Liverpool	24	13	6	5	44	20	45
Newcastle	24	11	9	4	41	25	42
Nottm Forest	25	12	6	7	37	28	42
Tottenham	24	11	6	7	41	35	39
Wimbledon	24	10	5	9	30	38	35
Leeds	23	9	7	7	29	27	34
Sheff Wed	25	8	9	8	31	32	33
Norwich	24	9	6	9	22	25	33
Arsenal	25	8	8	9	28	27	32
Chelsea	24	8	7	9	32	33	31
Man City	24	8	7	9	33	38	31
Aston Villa	25	6	10	9	31	35	28
Southampton	24	6	10	8	34	39	28
QPR	23	7	6	10	35	40	27
C Palace	25	6	8	11	18	25	26
Everton	24	6	8	10	25	33	26
Coventry	25	6	8	11	21	41	26
West Ham	24	7	4	13	22	30	25
Ipswich	25	5	5	15	28	49	20
Leicester	24	3	6	15	22	43	15

things even out during the year. But refereeing decisions have now gone against us in our last two meetings with United. Let us hope we get some breaks from now on. We certainly deserve them."

United boss Ferguson defended Durkin's decision. "It was clearly shown on TV that their player gave Keane a shove," he said. "If you are seeking an advantage and scoring a goal, what can a referee give? The official had his hand up right away. Kenny Dalglish said he wanted a strong ref for this game and he got his wish!

"He [Shearer] certainly gave our player a little shove. Look at the game overall and it would have been an absolute travesty if we hadn't won. It's given us a better chance in the championship race. I hope we now realise the importance of every game we have in future. We've been careless and lackadaisical recently."

Ferguson defended Cole's early miss. "It was a good chance but the important thing is he will be much better because we still won in his first United game. Another big plus was that he was caught offside only once in the whole 90 minutes."

Eric Cantona celebrates the late winner in style.

January 25

Eric Cantona, the heartbeat of Manchester United for the past two seasons, did the club he loves his greatest disservice by taking the law into his own hands at Selhurst Park. His temper snapped after being sent off for the fifth time in his United career and the borderline between genius and insanity shattered in a flurry of flying fists and feet.

Cantona, dismissed by referee Alan Wilkie in the 48th minute for kicking out at Palace's Richard Shaw, was taunted by a fan who ran down from 11 rows back in the main stand to hold up his middle finger.

Cantona should have walked on. Instead he lunged at the fan in a kung-fu kick with both feet off the ground and followed up with fists flailing.

Stewards intervened as the United players ran across to rescue their team-mate. Paul Ince along with Cantona, was charged by police. Cantona was led away in shame, a police superintendent at his heel. It all meant that United's drive towards the top of the Premiership hit an unexpected road block on an evening of frustration.

United could think themselves lucky that Palace's notoriously goal-shy forwards were unable to take advantage of their possession. In 25 league games Palace had scored only 18 goals, fewer than any other Premiership side. Only eight of them had come in 12 games at home.

Compare that to United's collective 46 goals and you know why they are reaching for the championship as Palace languish in the danger area.

The differential was not apparent early in the game as a pitch softened by the day's rain failed to provide the carpet for United's passing game. But Andy Cole, considered a penalty area player, proved there is more to his game as he threaded a fine through pass for Brian McClair but the ball bobbled on a divot.

Cole has now gone 10 games without a goal, providing the kind of pressure he could do without on his second appearance for United. His link-up play was impressive, but it was goals Alex Ferguson paid £7 million to see.

Ian Dowie, for whom Palace paid £6.6 million less, was the target

CRYSTAL PALACE 1
MANCHESTER UNITED 1
(Half-time score : 0-0)

Palace: Martyn, Gordon, Southgate, Coleman, Dowie (Preece 75), Armstrong, Salako, Shaw, Pitcher, Patterson, Newman.
United: Schmeichel, Irwin, Sharpe (Kanchelskis 83), Pallister, Cantona, Ince, McClair, Giggs, May, Keane, Cole.
Subs: Scholes, Walsh.
Scorers: (Palace): Southgate 79; (United): May 56.
Referee: A Wilkie (Chester le Street).
Attendance: 18,224

man for Palace. United had David May deputising for suspended skipper and central defender Steve Bruce.

There was an element of frustration in United's football as the pitch cut up. Palace were looking tight and nicely organised at the back, with Shaw conspicuous, and United's first real shot on goal came with a volley from McClair after Chris Coleman had headed out a Ryan Giggs free-kick.

The principal threat to United developed down the left flank where John Salako teased Roy Keane, deputising at right-back for the absent Paul Parker and Gary Neville. When Keane body-checked the tricky winger one time too many mid-way through the first half, Durham referee Wilkie showed the yellow card for the first time.

There was not the usual rhythm to United's football. Too many passes were not reaching their destination. Palace, in turn, were not making the most of their possession. Darren Pitcher tried to open up United's midfield but, when he did penetrate, Peter Schmeichel came out to the edge of his penalty area to deny Chris Armstrong.

The Palace centre-forward had a better chance six minutes from half-time after May flicked away a header. Salako's return cross to the far post was perfect for Armstrong but he directed the ball over the bar, typical of his form in the Premiership in which he has scored only twice in 25 games.

Salako should have scored in injury time, driving wide from 12 yards after Schmeichel had failed to clear a Darren Patterson cross under challenge from Armstrong.

David Davies, the FA's director of public affairs, said afterwards that the FA was appalled by the Cantona incident. "It brings shame on those involved as well as the game itself," he said. "The FA is aware that the police are urgently considering what action they should take. We will cooperate with them in every way.

"As far as the FA is concerned, charges of improper conduct and bringing the game into disrepute will inevitably and swiftly follow tonight's events. It is our responsibility to ensure that actions that damage the game are punished severely and the FA will live up to that responsibility."

League Table After Match

	P	W	D	L	F	A	Pts
Blackburn	25	18	4	3	56	20	58
Man Utd	26	16	6	4	47	21	54
Liverpool	25	13	7	5	44	20	46
Newcastle	25	12	9	4	43	26	45
Nottm Forest	26	13	6	7	39	28	45
Tottenham	25	11	6	8	41	36	39
Leeds	24	10	7	7	33	27	37
Sheff Wed	26	9	9	8	33	32	36
Wimbledon	25	10	5	10	31	40	35
Norwich	25	9	7	9	24	27	34
Arsenal	26	8	9	9	29	28	33
Aston Villa	26	7	10	9	32	35	31
Chelsea	25	8	7	10	32	35	31
Man City	25	8	7	10	33	39	31
Southampton	25	6	11	8	35	40	29
C Palace	26	6	9	11	19	26	27
Everton	25	6	9	10	25	33	27
QPR	24	7	6	11	35	44	27
Coventry	26	6	9	11	23	43	27
West Ham	25	7	4	14	22	32	25
Ipswich	26	5	5	16	29	53	20
Leicester	25	4	6	15	23	43	18

January 28

The Old Trafford faithful offered an extraordinary outpouring of forgiveness for Eric Cantona's split personality. They chanted his name endlessly, exonerating his trespasses at Crystal Palace and suggesting that the beauty he had bestowed on the game atoned for everything.

Cantona stayed well away from the match but he would have revelled in the generous spaces Wrexham offered in a Cup tie United won with ease.

The crowd indulged their repertoire of Cantona chants throughout the afternoon and it proved an inspiring battle anthem for the United players left to pick up the pieces of a remarkable week.

A Cup tie away from the intensity of the Premiership campaign was just what United and their fans needed after the events of last week; and the Welsh side provided interesting opposition, bringing to the occasion an attacking philosophy not dissimilar to that of their hosts.

An early Wrexham goal reminded United that they could not afford to sulk. Ferguson said afterwards: "I thought what had happened last week would bring the best out of us and it did. We looked very sharp and bright. Our attacking options were always good and, though we could have lost more goals, we might have scored more."

Denied Cantona, the suspended Bruce and the injured Hughes and Kanchelskis, Ferguson was able to introduce another of his seemingly endless supply of talented young players and this time Philip Neville showed the benefits of a good Old Trafford education.

Paul Scholes stepped into the Cantona void, which is roughly like asking a boy soprano to take over from Pavarotti. But the little Mancunian performed, with huge credit in difficult circumstances.

Lee Sharpe, Roy Keane, and above all, Ryan Giggs began to show an edge and a confidence in their game which is reassuring. Andrei Kanchelskis continued his rehabilitation as a second-half substitute.

Ferguson said: "Giggs looked as if he was enjoying himself. He was running at opponents' legs again. We brought him back because we need him. His fitness will come gradually.

"Sharpe is looking better and when he is fully match fit he will start scoring goals. Giggs has had to put up with a lot of unfair scrutiny.

MANCHESTER UNITED 5

WREXHAM 2

(Half-time score : 2-1)

United: Schmeichel, Neville, Irwin, May, Sharpe, Pallister, Keane (Kanchelskis 69), Ince, McClair (Beckham 73), Scholes, Giggs.
Sub: Walsh.
Wrexham: Marriott, Jones, Hardy, Hughes (Phillips 80), Hunter, Humes, Bennett, Owen, Connolly (Cross 71), Watkin, Durkan.
Scorers: (United): Irwin 17, Giggs 26, McClair 67, Humes 73 pen, 80 og. (Wrexham): Durkan 10, Cross 89.
Referee: M J Bodenham (East Looe).
Attendance: 43,222

Don't forget that he is still only 21. It's good to see him looking more like his old self again."

Wrexham's early goal came from Kieron Durkan, the 21-year-old winger who volleyed one of the goals that sent Ipswich spinning out of the competition in the third round.

Popping up on the left as Wrexham continued their spirited opening, Durkan swapped passes with Gareth Owen before firing wide of Peter Schmeichel's left hand.

Denis Irwin, who had been pig in the middle as Wrexham worked their goalscoring move, quickly hammered an equaliser from a Giggs corner. The debutant Neville, 18, had an important part in the second goal, which was side-footed home by Giggs for only his third of the season.

Neville, as lively at left-back as Scholes was in United's new-look attack, thumped a post before half-time and Gary Pallister headed against the bar soon afterwards.

Wrexham would not lie down and Schmeichel had to make three world-class saves from Durkan, Barry Hunter and Steve Watkin before United ran away with the game.

Their class eventually told with Brian McClair scoring sweetly from Pallister's lay-off, Irwin converting a penalty and Humes turning a cross from Giggs beyond his own goalkeeper Andy Marriott.

Wrexham grabbed a second in the dying seconds when substitute Jonathan Cross beat Schmeichel with a deflected shot.

Giggs gives Irvin a Hi-5 after Irwin's goal for United.

February 4

Alex Ferguson, banking on the feel-good factor to inspire Manchester United's defence of the Double, may well look back on the politically popular U-turn over Mark Hughes as the crucial moment of their season.

After two weeks of turmoil in the wake of the Eric Cantona affair, suddenly Old Trafford was awash with smiling faces. Hughes had the new two-year contract he had always demanded as the price of staying, and Andy Cole scored his first match-winning goal for the club after his £7 million transfer.

The fans crowed with joy over both. Grinning in the middle of it all, Ferguson could sense optimism flooding back through the club and see genuine hope of defending both the Championship and FA Cup.

This victory over reviving Villa was fortunate. Honest eyes saw that. But winning three points despite playing poorly was evidence of deep resilience, argued Ferguson, who then explained the significance of the Hughes deal.

He said: "We changed our thinking on Mark. We felt all the controversy over the past two weeks had had a detrimental effect on the spirits of everyone at the club. We wanted to give the supporters, in particular, some good news.

"Then it was wonderful to see Andy score. I'm glad he's got this early goal because not getting one has destroyed careers here in the past."

What will be crucial now is whether the Hughes-Cole combination can click in the way that Beardsley-Cole and Hughes-Cantona did.

United openly admitted they bought Englishman Cole to feed off the sublime passing of Cantona, willing to discard Welshman Hughes because of problems with the foreigners rule in European competition.

Many critics, beginning with Alan Hansen on *Match of the Day*, fear Cole and Hughes might not be so productive a partnership.

Hughes, speaking with the calm authority of a striker with true international stature, believes they will gel. He has to believe it because he knows that, if it does not work, he will be the player to lose his place at the club, crowd hero or not.

Signatures on a piece of paper do not prevent wars, never mind

MANCHESTER UNITED 1

ASTON VILLA 0

(Half-time score : 1-0)

United: Schmeichel, Neville (May 64), Irwin, Bruce, Sharpe, Pallister, Scholes, Ince, McClair, Cole, Giggs (Kanchelskis44).
Sub: Walsh.
Villa: Bosnich, Charles, Staunton, Teale, McGrath, Small, Yorke (Houghton 61), Fashanu (Johnson 43), Saunders, Taylor, Townsend.
Scorers: Cole 18.
Referee: D Elleray (Harrow).
Attendance: 43,795

popular footballers being transferred on a whim. The 31-year-old Welshman admitted: "The crowd helped me get the contract, there's no doubt about that. The electorate at Old Trafford voted for me. A week ago I was very close to leaving the club – but a week's a long time in football, as they say.

"The idea had been to play Eric and Andy, and I'm not one to hang around without first-team football. I had a meeting with the club on Friday, and it's fair to say that, if they hadn't been willing to talk about the two-year contract, I would have been going.

"I'm delighted that it's all over and done with. I feel a lot happier in myself. I've just moved house on Thursday. The contract happened on Friday. Everything is falling into place.

"Now I've got to try to make an impression with Andy and hopefully give the manager something to think about next year. I think I can play with him. Andy is the type of forward who plays on a defender's shoulders, whereas I'm more a sort of link player. I think it could be a good combination. Hopefully I can play him in a lot.

"We have different qualities that can upset defenders, his pace and my strength for example. And the more problems you can give the opposing team the better chance you've got.

"The goal today will do Andy the world of good, breaking that barrier. It took me five games to score at the start. It's difficult and it's vital."

Cole spun sharply inside the six-yard box to volley home a downward header from Gary Pallister in the 18th minute – a classic poacher's goal.

And the former Newcastle striker showed his commitment to the cause, too, by playing almost the entire 90 minutes with his left eye battered closed like a boxer's.

Cole said: "We have to knuckle down together after what's happened. Of course we'll miss Eric. But we are determined to win the Championship and, if we do, it will be for Eric as well.

"Now I'm really looking forward to playing with Sparky. He's a class striker. Everybody knows how good he is, and that's why the supporters want him to stay. Hopefully we'll be a good combination."

League Table After Match

	P	W	D	L	F	A	Pts
Blackburn	26	18	5	3	57	21	59
Man Utd	27	17	6	4	48	21	57
Newcastle	27	13	9	5	45	29	48
Liverpool	26	13	8	5	45	21	47
Nottm Forest	27	13	7	7	40	29	46
Leeds	26	10	9	7	34	28	39
Tottenham	25	11	6	8	41	36	39
Sheff Wed	27	10	9	8	36	33	39
Wimbledon	26	10	6	10	31	40	36
Norwich	26	9	7	10	25	29	34
Arsenal	27	8	9	10	30	31	33
Chelsea	26	8	8	10	34	37	32
Man City	26	8	8	10	35	41	32
Aston Villa	27	7	10	10	32	36	31
Southampton	26	6	12	8	37	42	30
C Palace	27	7	9	11	31	26	30
QPR	25	8	6	11	38	44	30
Everton	27	7	9	11	27	36	30
West Ham	26	8	4	14	24	33	28
Coventry	27	6	10	11	25	45	28
Ipswich	27	5	5	17	29	55	20
Leicester	26	4	6	16	24	45	18

Villa, one of the clubs who had kept a close eye this season on the Hughes contract saga at Old Trafford, should have taken at least a point from this match after dominating possession. They have improved immeasurably in recent weeks under the leadership of Brian Little and relegation ought not to be a concern by May.

Dean Saunders hit the bar with one swerving volley and Tommy Johnson might have had a hat-trick with more composure in front of goal.

But on this day fortune was finally smiling on United.

Cole scores winner and first goal for United.

February 11

MANCHESTER CITY 0

MANCHESTER UNITED 3

(Half-time score : 0-0)

City: Dibble, Summerbee, D
Brightwell, Gaudino, Curle,
Kernaghan, I Brightwell, Walsh,
Rosler, Flitcroft, Beagrie (Quinn
63).
United: Schmeichel, Irwin, Bruce,
Sharpe, Pallister, Ince, McClair,
Giggs, Kanchelskis (May 82),
Cole, Neville (Scholes 53).
Sub: Walsh.
Scorers: Ince 58, Kanchelskis 74,
Cole 77.
Referee: P Don (Hamworth
Park).
Attendance: 26,368

When Alex Ferguson paid a jackpot for Andy Cole it was not a gamble on how many goals he might score as much as a belief there was much more in his locker. The week he joined United, Chris Sutton was asked what he felt about Cole and he said: "The quickest feet I have seen."

Cole might have had a disruptive season with shin splints, goal droughts and an inflated transfer fee but at Maine Road he used those Fred Astaire feet to spectacular effect. In the space of a week Cole has wiped off the early installments with a crucial goal against Aston Villa and a winning contribution to swamp City.

There were enlightening indications of a rapport with Ryan Giggs which could be the cornerstone of United's drive for a third successive Premiership. Cole seemed to understand where to position himself in relation to Giggs, using the left flank intelligently when the Welshman went on those energising, exhilarating runs.

With Andrei Kanchelskis' pace also returning to near Olympic sprint levels, and Paul Ince herding his team-mates like a cattle driver, there is suddenly a new urgency about United.

Fergie clearly senses the next few matches are going to be critical in what is looking more than ever like a two-horse race with Blackburn. "This is the stage where you know that to lose or to draw means something," he said. "You do a bit of shadow-boxing for a lot of the season and you can be a bit careless. We were like that in some of our away fixtures. We lost three goals at Ipswich, two at Leeds, two at Chelsea and two at Southampton. . . and you can't go on doing that."

He added: "We were not careless defensively against City. Steve Bruce and Gary Pallister were terrific and so was Peter Schmeichel when he was needed. If they do that then we will get goals the other end. The boy Cole will score goals, especially away from home where there tends to be more space. And now we have Kanchelskis back and Giggs starting to go, we can push on."

City, of course, have been good for United's goal difference column this season; eight in two games without reply. But Fergie was content enough not to exert more pressure on Brian Horton than already exists. The City manager acknowledged United's superiority, saying:

"Nobody would have put that scoreline down at half-time. But that's what they are – the best team around. The central defenders were outstanding."

Bruce summed it up when he said: "Once we scored we ran all over the top of them. They started to leave a lot of space and our lads up front just love that. Maybe we have not been as fluent as last season but there is real resilience among this mob. They are a tough load of characters and they want to succeed. And the flow is coming back."

Andy Cole celebrates his goal with McClair and Giggs.

League Table After Match

	P	W	D	L	F	A	Pts
Blackburn	28	19	5	4	61	25	62
Man Utd	28	18	6	4	51	21	60
Newcastle	28	14	9	5	47	30	51
Liverpool	27	13	9	5	46	22	48
Nottm Forrest	28	13	7	8	41	31	46
Tottenham	27	12	7	8	45	38	43
Leeds	26	10	9	7	34	28	39
Sheff Wed	29	10	9	10	38	38	39
Aston Villa	29	9	10	10	41	38	37
Wimbledon	27	10	6	11	32	47	36
Norwich	27	9	8	10	27	31	35
Arsenal	28	8	10	10	31	32	34
Coventry	29	8	10	11	29	45	34
Chelsea	27	8	9	10	35	38	33
Man City	27	8	8	11	35	44	32
Southampton	27	6	13	8	39	44	31
QPR	26	8	7	11	39	45	31
Everton	28	7	10	11	29	38	31
C Palace	28	7	9	12	21	28	30
West Ham	28	8	5	15	26	37	29
Ipswich	27	5	5	17	29	55	20
Leicester	27	4	7	16	25	46	19

February 19

MANCHESTER UNITED 3

LEEDS 1

(Half-time score : 2-0)

United: Schmeichel, Keane, Irwin, Bruce, Sharpe, Pallister, Kanchelskis, Ince, McClair, Hughes, Giggs.
Subs: Butt, Scholes, Walsh
Leeds: Lukic, Kelly, Dorigo, Whelan, Pemberton, Wetherall, White, Wallace (Worthington 45), Masinga (Yeboah 45), McAllister, Speed.
Scorers: (United): Bruce 1, McClair 4, Hughes 72; (Leeds): Yeboah 53.
Referee: M D Reed (Birmingham).
Attendance: 42,744

Mark Hughes, who thought his Manchester United career had been laid to rest, underwent the kind of resurrection normally associated with another form of Sunday worship.

Leeds United had hauled themselves back from conceding two sloppy goals in the first four minutes of this FA Cup fifth-round tie at Old Trafford and were threatening a dramatic revival when Sparky's fuse was ignited. The header he steered beyond the groping left hand of John Lukic did much more than finally demoralise an old enemy. It was an emphatic statement that United intend to be the first side to achieve the double Double.

The draw that gives them a home quarter-final against Queens Park Rangers does nothing to detract from their conviction that the Theatre of Dreams can the the Realm of Reality. Hughes, of course, is a symbol to the fans of United in much the same way that Eric Cantona has been, and idolatry is something of an occupational hazard at this club.

Yet this victory owed most to the Trojan work of two of the club's revered workers: Brian McClair and Roy Keane. To outpower Leeds United it is essential to cancel out the creativity of Gary McAllister and Gary Speed, an exercise the United midfield achieved with a vigorous mix of industry and expertise.

If the loss of Carlton Palmer and Brian Deane through suspension was not enough, Leeds had to accept first-half contributions from Danny Wallace and Phil Masinga which were a defamation of their profession. Only when they were withdrawn for more honest toilers in Nigel Worthington and Anthony Yeboah did Leeds look like forming even a token impediment towards United's progress.

In the end it was only the courageous intervention of the veteran John Lukic who prevented this becoming the kind of scoreline that sends football managers reaching for a bottle of sleeping pills.

To offer Manchester United a two-goal start, indeed, is roughly like a general flying the white flag before a bullet has been fired. But this is what Leeds did.

David Weatherall floored Hughes in the first few seconds of the game and from Denis Irwin's free-kick Noel Whelan conceded a corner.

There were 63 seconds on the clock as Ryan Giggs whipped in the cross and Masinga stayed glued to terra firma as Steve Bruce soared superbly to direct a powerful header past Lukic.

If that was bad enough, worse was to follow three minutes later as Giggs crossed to the right to take another corner. This time Gary Pallister flicked it back at the near post and there was McClair saying thank-you for the space.

"Two-Nil Without Cantona," the delirious among the 42,744 chorused and so complete was United's command that they began to perform pretty patterns of keep-ball. Fifteen, 16, 17, passes at a time were exchanged as Leeds hid behind the ball as if the grip of fear prevented them stepping out of their own penalty area. That kind of cowering is an open invitation to men like Andrei Kanchelskis and Giggs to run you ragged and United's flyers, both back on full jet power, tore away at them.

Leeds came out regrouped for the second half and in the 53rd minute substitute Yeboah pulled them back into it. Kanchelskis had forced Lukic into a spectacular save, tipping a ferocious drive from a short free-kick on to his crossbar, when Leeds caught United on a quick break.

It was a scrambled goal, mis-hit from three yards from David White's centre, but it counted and suddenly Leeds saw a glimmer of hope and White flashed a shot just wide of Peter Schmeichel's goal.

When Keane and Ince combined to put Kanchelskis in down the right in the 72nd minute, it was a relief for United. The ball into the centre was perfect and Hughes steered it home expertly. It was an emotional moment for him and his fans and he described it later as the start of a Second Coming.

Then it might have been more, Lukic denying Kanchelskis with real gallantry and making an even more heroic save as Giggs ghosted into the heart of the area. Ince headed off the line from Speed but the last gesture of the game was from Kanchelskis, scooping the ball over the bar from a Giggs cross.

By then it did not matter. The fans had witnessed the reincarnation of their hero and he, in return, had delivered them from their anxiety. Hughes said: "Everyone, the fans and my team-mates knew exactly how I felt when I scored. It was an emotional moment for me because if things had been different then I might never have been here today. I had come to the conclusion that for the good of my career I would have to move, but I am delighted to still be part of this great club.

"It felt like a new beginning for me and for the first game in a long time I felt really nervous running out. I was so keen to make an impact because the supporters have been coming up to me in the street and making it clear that they wanted me to stay.

"The goal was a big thank-you to all of them. This club just gets bigger and bigger and it is the only place to be."

Fergie said: "Mark has demonstrated over the years what a big-game player he is and he has proved it again by scoring such an important goal. This club has a history of building legends. Sparky has been a hero for 10 years."

Steve Bruce heads United's third.

February 22

Alex Ferguson's bold attacking policy paid rich dividends as Manchester United kept up the title pressure on Blackburn. But the jury remained out on the vital question for United's dream of retaining the double: will the Andy Cole-Mark Hughes partnership gel?

They certainly failed to click at Carrow Road as United relied on early goals from Paul Ince and Andrei Kanchelskis to overcome spirited Norwich. Too often the pair made identical runs, almost colliding in their eagerness to be the focus of moves inspired by Ince.

Of course it would be foolish to judge them on only one match in unison but Ferguson knows there is little time to forge a dynamic partnership as Blackburn continue to win. "We hardly got the ball up to the front pair," he said, "so it was impossible to assess them tonight. I think Peter Schmeichel got more passes from midfield than they did."

This was a night when United could have significantly improved their goal difference with a sharper end product.

The United manager had set the tone by adventurously selecting Roy Keane and Lee Sharpe as his full-backs, dropping Denis Irwin for the first time this season.

There was immediate reward with a goal after two minutes 43 seconds, and that after Norwich had announced their own intentions with Mike Sheron forcing a brilliant save from Schmeichel.

United's strike came from a corner poorly cleared by Norwich skipper Jon Newsome. His header fell to Ince, 20 yards from goal, and the England star volleyed into the net.

Ashley Ward headed against the bar as Norwich, trying to put a 5-0 FA Cup defeat at Everton behind them, responded with invention. But United clinched the points with a clinical counter-attack from their own penalty area in the 16th minute.

Ince's header clear was quickly passed on by Hughes and Brian McClair for Ryan Giggs to speed forward through a vacant midfield. The young Welshman had options right and left and chose wisely in releasing Kanchelskis to zoom in from the right wing and score with a low shot past the unprotected Andy Marshall.

Giggs wasted subsequent good positions with poor control,

NORWICH 0

MANCHESTER UNITED 2

(Half-time score : 0-2)

Norwich: Marshall, Bradshaw, Bowen, Newsome, Polston, Adams, Milligan, Johnson, Ward, Sheron, Eadie.
United: Schmeichel, Keane, Sharpe, Pallister, Ince, Kanchelskis, Bruce, McClair, Cole, Hughes, Giggs.
Subs: Irwin, Butt, Walsh.
Scorers: Ince 2, Kanchelskis 16.
Referee: Worrall (Warrington).
Attendance: 21,824

although the swirling wind and rain was hardly conducive to one-touch football. But he did provide Cole with his only chance of the match in the 34th minute.

The striker, looking for the 100th senior goal of his career, chested down the cross but, as he prepared to shoot, John Polston nicked the ball away for a corner. It symbolised a frustrating night for the £7 million man and Hughes, who appeared to be denied a second-half penalty when tripped in the box.

Victory made it 13 matches unbeaten for United, who remain two points behind Blackburn. Norwich, in contrast, have won once in nine games and are in danger of dropping into the relegation dogfight. On this evidence they appear too good to go down, keeping United at full stretch for 90 minutes without quite having the penetration to make second-half pressure tell.

Gary Pallister and Roy Keane were lucky to escape bookings, but the use of Keane at right-back looks a useful policy by Ferguson. He dealt admirably with the hostility of the crowd and the venomous pace and skill of Norwich's highly rated winger Darren Eadie.

"We are at the ticklish stage of the season where nobody can afford any mistakes," said Ferguson. "The club which makes fewest errors is the one which wins things. Our performance tonight was economical. There was a safety element, keeping the ball in midfield when we might have got it forward.

"But our players have valuable experience after two years of winning the title. They know what to do and I sense they are getting better and better. We know what wins titles. It is luck, ability, concentration, determination and desire."

League Table After Match

	P	W	D	L	F	A	Pts
Blackburn	29	20	5	4	63	26	65
Man Utd	29	19	6	4	53	21	63
Newcastle	28	14	9	5	47	30	51
Liverpool	27	13	9	5	46	22	48
Nottm Forest	29	13	7	9	41	32	46
Tottenham	27	12	7	8	45	38	43
Leeds	27	11	9	7	35	28	42
Sheff Wed	29	10	9	10	38	48	39
Aston Villa	30	9	11	10	45	42	38
Arsenal	29	9	10	10	32	32	37
Wimbledon	28	10	6	12	33	49	36
Norwich	28	9	8	11	27	33	35
Man City	28	9	8	11	37	44	35
Coventry	29	8	10	11	29	45	34
Chelsea	27	8	9	10	35	38	33
Southampton	27	6	13	8	39	44	31
QPR	26	8	7	11	39	45	31
Everton	29	7	10	12	29	39	31
C Palace	28	7	9	12	21	28	30
West Ham	28	8	5	15	26	37	29
Leicester	28	4	8	16	29	50	20
Ipswich	28	5	5	18	29	57	20

February 25

Beaming Everton manager Joe Royle detached himself briefly from his own superlatives about Duncan Ferguson to throw down a challenge to United's conqueror. "He should be getting 25 to 30 goals a season," said Royle after Ferguson, Everton's £4 million cult hero, put United to the sword with a classic far-post header from a typically lethal Andy Hinchcliffe corner.

Ferguson's eighth goal in his last eight home outings – he has yet to score away – was the crowning glory of Royle's tactical triumph.

With United manager Ferguson leaving Andrei Kanchelskis on the bench, unleashing him only when the champions were chasing the game, Royle won the points and the battle of wits with his friend from Old Trafford.

He sent towering target man Ferguson into battle as a lone striker, serviced by a five-man midfield, with Stuart Barlow raiding on the right and Anders Limpar on the left. Hamstring victim Graham Stuart's absence gave Barlow a rare start and the former butcher who cost nothing outshone £7 million Andy Cole and Ryan Giggs.

Royle's formation brought Everton's first home goal against United since September 1989, in front of their first 40,000-plus league crowd since that same month.

Everton's success was aided and abetted by errant finishing from Cole and Mark Hughes, whose failings were due both to their own inaccuracy and to Neville Southall's positioning. "We had five really good chances and if we'd taken one we would have won the match," said disappointed manager Ferguson.

But the role of match-winner fell to his Everton namesake in the 58th minute and the big striker is now being mentioned in the same breath as the most glittering of Goodison glitterati. While the player himself continued his self-imposed vow of silence Royle, who took the decision to sign the controversial star from Rangers, told *Match of the Day* viewers: "Duncan's a legend already on Merseyside and if he continues at this rate he's going to be the biggest thing at Everton since Alex Young."

By the time the manager had ascended to the Goodison press room the comparisons had risen with him. "Duncan could be the biggest

EVERTON 1
MANCHESTER UNITED 0
(Half-time score : 0-0)

Everton: Southall, Barrett, Watson, Unsworth, Hinchcliffe, Ebbrell (Samways 71), Horne, Parkinson, Limpar, Ferguson, Barlow.
United: Schmeichel, Irwin, Bruce, Pallister, Sharpe, Ince, Keane, McClair (Kanchelskis 66), Giggs, Cole, Hughes.
Subs: Butt, Walsh.
Scorer: Ferguson 58.
Referee: J Worrall (Warrington).
Attendance: 40,011

thing here since Dixie Dean," bubbled Royle, "I mean that".

"The fans love him. He's massive. He's the Prime Minister of Merseyside. It's adulation in a big way and he's looking cheap at the price."

Royle could not contain his enthusiasm for the Scot. "He's not just a lamp-post; he can play as well. He's got a deft touch and he has pace."

But then Royle, himself one of Everton's distinguished No 9s, set a goal target for his prized possession, whose best seasonal output was 17 for Dundee United in the 1991-92 season. "He isn't a natural goalscorer," said Royle. "If he starts getting scrappy goals as well as the sharp ones, he'll really be up there among them. He should be capable of 25 to 30 a season, expecting mistakes from defenders and looking for chances. He's got the basics to go all the way. He can take anyone on."

Team-mate Barry Horne, who rivalled skipper Dave Watson as man of the match, was more impressed by Ferguson's performance than his jubilant shirt-waving act after scoring. "Rehearsed celebrations do my head in quite frankly, although I think that one was spontaneous," said the Wales captain, an inspiration in midfield against Paul Ince and Co.

"Duncan has this thing about him that all great players have – presence – and at 23 he can be one of the game's greats. I'm not saying he doesn't apply himself all the time now but, when he matures and becomes more knowledgeable, he'll be even better."

Gary Pallister and Steve Bruce never looked comfortable against their towering Everton foe. And United manager Ferguson conceded his namesake's punishment of Peter Schmeichel's failure to reach Hinchcliffe's corner was one of the big threats Everton posed.

"Hinchcliffe does rocket them in and they are very difficult to defend," said Fergie. "But it was a bad goal from our point of view and we're not happy with it. I thought we defended well apart from that.

"Ferguson is a handful and quite mobile for a big lad. He'll give a lot of teams a hard time. But I think we coped as well as I expected us to. He was up against the two best centre-backs in the country."

League Table After Match

	P	W	D	L	F	A	Pts
Blackburn	30	20	6	4	63	26	66
Man Utd	30	19	6	5	53	22	63
Newcastle	29	15	9	5	50	31	54
Liverpool	28	14	9	5	48	23	51
Nottm Forest	30	13	8	9	42	33	47
Leeds	28	11	10	7	35	28	43
Tottenham	28	12	7	9	46	40	43
Arsenal	30	10	10	10	35	32	40
Sheff Wed	30	10	9	11	39	40	39
Wimbledon	29	11	6	12	35	50	39
Aston Villa	31	9	11	11	46	45	38
Coventry	30	9	10	11	33	47	37
Chelsea	28	9	9	10	37	39	36
Norwich	29	9	9	11	27	33	36
Man City	29	9	9	11	37	44	36
Everton	30	8	10	12	30	39	34
QPR	27	8	8	11	40	46	32
Southampton	28	6	13	9	40	46	31
C Palace	29	7	9	13	21	31	30
West Ham	29	8	5	16	27	39	29
Ipswich	29	6	5	18	31	58	23
Leicester	29	4	8	17	31	54	20

March 4

As the riskiest investment in British football, Andy Cole has been desperate to prove his was one multi-million deal that had not lost its barings. Seven games, seven goals and suddenly Alex Ferguson's £7 million gamble is paying back a lucrative rate of interest in the one currency that matters: goals.

As the sceptics debated whether canny Kevin Keegan knew something the rest of football did not about his prolific striker, Ferguson has been telling anyone prepared to listen that his expensive recruit "is capable of anything".

The greatest scoring performance in Manchester United's 103-year league history, a five-goal feat to elevate him above Best, Law and Charlton, proved it.

For Cole goals mean confidence and his looked rock bottom after seven minutes when, clean through, he reduced Old Trafford's biggest crowd of the season to stunned silence by treading on the ball and falling flat on his face.

An hour and a half later he was clutching the match ball to his chest, the crowd were singing "Swing low, sweet Andy Cole" and the beaming smile as he trooped off to a standing ovation meant one thing: Goal King Cole is back in business.

The striker, who claimed his 100th senior goal at the age of 23 with his first strike of the afternoon, said: "I can only get better and I've got five years here to do it. I came to Old Trafford to play with the best players in the country and now I'm starting to realise just how good they are.

"It was the most complete team performance I've ever been involved in. It was a 10 out of 10 and if the manager says that was the closest he's ever seen to perfection I'm happy to agree.

"Everyone has been asking whether I'm worth £7 million, and saying I am this or that. I've scored five today and it's all OK. But I might not score next week and people will probably start saying I'm a waste of money. That doesn't bother me because I don't feel I've got to prove anything except to the manager and the supporters. I'm thrilled because I've never scored five in a match in my life. Hopefully now they'll keep flowing."

MANCHESTER UNITED 9
IPSWICH 0
(Half-time score : 3-0)

United: Schmeichel, Keane (Sharpe 45), Irwin, Bruce (Butt 80), Kanchelskis, Pallister, Cole, Ince, McClair, Hughes, Giggs. *Sub:* Walsh.
Ipswich: Forest, Yallop, Thompson, Wark, Linighan, Palmer, Williams, Sedgley, Slater, Mathie, Chapman (Marshall 64).
Scorers: Keane 15, Cole 19, 37, 53, 65, 87, Hughes 55, 59, Ince 72.
Referee: G Poll (Tilehurst).
Attendance: 43,804

Irresistible, merciless and mesmerising as they were, United could not have pulled off the biggest win in the history of the Premiership without a bit of help from their friends. Ipswich seemed more than happy to assist.

A back four with a combined age of 128, including 37-year-old daddy of the league John Wark, creaked and groaned as United's kids ran amok. Ipswich did not lose just the 50-50 tackles but the 70-30 ones as well.

Any sympathy they might have expected for an appalling decision that allowed Paul Ince to chip a free-kick into an empty net for United's eighth as keeper Craig Forest was still being booked had long since been cast aside by a performance that should ensure their own slot in the record books: the limpest performance in history.

Manager George Burley was too shell-shocked to talk about it, his players were presumably too ashamed.

For the record, and there were plenty of those at Old Trafford including United's biggest league win since the 10-1 trouncing of Wolves in 1892, it could have been virtually however many United wanted it to be.

Roy Keane opened the scoring on 15 minutes with a low drive and then Cole took over. He doubled the lead four minutes later with a brilliant sliding finish to Ryan Giggs' low cross, grabbed his second on 37 minutes, when a Mark Hughes overhead volley crashed back off the bar and landed at his feet, and finished his hat-trick eight minutes after the restart with a far-post header.

Hughes grabbed the best of the lot with a far-post blast for the fifth, headed the sixth when Forest could only deflect a Giggs shot and watched Cole whip in the seventh.

Ince's cheeky free-kick routine was number eight and Cole turned and blasted in from close range for number nine.

The game had long since turned into a carnival, Mexican waves and all, but there was a serious side to the fun and games: goal difference.

Hughes has been around football too long to get carried away by one performance, however good, and his note of warning will no doubt be repeated by Fergie before what is sure to be a sterner test at Wimbledon.

The Welshman claimed: "It was one of those special days, one that people will probably be telling their grandchildren about and saying 'I was there'.

"The last time I was involved in a nine-goal win was at school. You just don't expect results like that in the Premiership, even against struggling sides. It was an exceptional performance.

"But the most important thing now is that our goal difference is better than Blackburn's. In the past we might have been guilty of messing about and showboating but the boss told us at half-time when we were 3-0 up not to take our foot off the pedal."

League Table After Match

	P	W	D	L	F	A	Pts
Blackburn	31	21	6	4	64	26	69
Man Utd	31	20	6	5	62	22	66
Newcastle	31	16	9	6	52	33	57
Liverpool	29	15	9	5	50	23	54
Nottm Forest	31	13	9	9	44	35	48
Tottenham	29	12	8	9	48	42	44
Leeds	29	11	10	8	35	29	43
Sheff Wed	31	11	9	11	40	40	42
Arsenal	31	10	10	11	35	33	40
Wimbledon	30	11	6	13	36	53	39
Aston Villa	32	9	11	12	46	46	38
Coventry	31	9	11	11	33	47	38
Chelsea	29	9	10	10	37	39	37
Norwich	30	9	10	11	28	34	37
Man City	30	9	10	11	38	45	37
QPR	28	9	8	11	43	47	35
Everton	31	8	11	12	32	41	35
Southampton	29	6	14	9	40	46	32
West Ham	30	9	5	16	28	39	32
C Palace	30	7	10	13	21	31	31
Ipswich	31	6	5	20	31	69	23
Leicester	30	4	9	17	33	56	21

Mark Hughes scores his second and United's 8th goal.

March 7

WIMBLEDON 0
MANCHESTER UNITED 1
(Half-time score : 0-0)

Wimbledon: Segers, Barton, Jones, Holdsworth, Elkins, Kimble, Gayle (Ardley 84), Perry, Goodman, Reeves, Cunningham.
United: Schmeichel, Irwin, Bruce, Sharpe, Pallister, Ince, McClair, Hughes, Giggs, Cole, Neville.
Subs: Davies, Casper, Walsh.
Scorer: Bruce 84.
Referee: R Hart (Darlington).
Attendance: 18,224

Manchester United took over as Premiership leaders amid controversy and touchline chaos. Wimbledon manager Joe Kinnear was ordered off the bench and club owner Sam Hammam clashed with police.

Steve Bruce's 84th-minute winner had prompted the bitter scenes around the Wimbledon dug-out. But it was the sending-off of Alan Kimble a little earlier that sparked the row. Kinnear confronted referee Robbie Hart, who was called a "muppet" by Arsenal's Ian Wright earlier this season.

"He ordered me off the pitch in his normal Hitler fashion," Kinnear said. "He was a dreadful referee and I know I've got myself into trouble again. But we have to put up with these people week in and week out."

Kimble had gone for his second bookable offence – encroaching on a corner – as United looked like being held and missing the chance to take over at the top. "How can a player be sent off after being just nine yards away from a corner?" added Kinnear.

The winner came after Wimbledon goalkeeper Hans Segers had fumbled a cross from Brian McClair allowing Bruce to put the ball into the net. "The goalkeeper made a bloomer," said Kinnear. "I had no complaints about the goal but it was the tough end of the stick to get the player sent off. We had limited them to just two shots all evening."

United boss Alex Ferguson sympathised: "It was a lucky victory. They deserved a draw. We didn't create anything." Ferguson admitted he had had second thoughts about selecting England midfielder Paul Ince, charged the previous day with assault at the same ground during the infamous Eric Cantona attack on a Crystal Palace fan. "I had reservations but we were down to the bare bones," said Ferguson. "Something always seems to happen when we come here but it was a quieter night for us than the last visit."

Ferguson had pushed Bruce forward in a last-ditch effort to break the resistance of Wimbledon's defence. There seemed no danger when Brian McClair lifted a hopeful ball towards the penalty area. Goalkeeper Hans Segers seemed to have it comfortably in his sights but, like a fielder squinting into the sun, he fumbled the catch and Bruce was on hand to squeeze it through his legs. Kinnear, already fuming at Kimble's red card, dashed on to the pitch, apparently to protest that the ball had been kicked from Segers' hands.

The cloying mud of a pitch had been passed fit only after three inspections by Hart. Wimbledon, hit by injuries, made no serious effort to win the game, setting out their battle plan to mark man-for-man, to stifle and frustrate and to pick up what they could.

Yet they might have taken the lead through a mental lapse by Denis Irwin. The United full-back lobbed a throw-in straight to the feet of Wimbledon's lone striker Dean Holdsworth and he ought to have scored, rolling the ball across the face of United's goal before young Gary Neville cleared.

United's first strike on target came from Neville, a superb shot from outside the area, and Segers needed an acrobatic leap to his right to keep it out.

Then Tony Gayle, who looked the most dangerous forward on the field, was through one on one with Peter Schmeichel. The Dane blocked his first shot and, when Gayle lobbed the rebound over the United keeper, Gary Pallister had recovered his position to head off the line.

Kimble went off in the 80th minute, Bruce was pushed forward and with six minutes left, the fateful ball was delivered by McClair and the fingers of fate were those of the hapless Segers.

League Table After Match

	P	W	D	L	F	A	Pts
Blackburn	33	22	7	4	68	28	73
Man Utd	32	21	6	5	63	22	69
Newcastle	32	17	9	6	54	33	60
Liverpool	29	15	9	5	50	23	54
Nottm Forrest	33	15	9	9	50	38	54
Tottenham	30	13	8	9	51	42	47
Leeds	30	12	10	8	38	29	46
Sheff Wed	33	11	10	12	40	41	43
Wimbledon	32	12	6	14	37	54	42
Arsenal	32	10	10	12	36	36	40
Chelsea	31	10	10	11	39	43	40
Coventry	33	9	13	11	34	48	40
Aston Villa	33	9	12	12	46	46	39
Norwich	32	9	12	11	30	36	39
QPR	29	10	8	11	45	47	38
Man City	31	9	10	12	39	47	37
Everton	32	8	11	13	33	43	35
West Ham	32	9	6	17	30	43	33
Southampton	29	6	14	9	40	46	32
C Palace	30	7	10	13	21	31	31
Ipswich	32	6	5	21	31	72	23
Leicester	32	4	9	19	35	62	21

Bruce makes Segers pay for his fumble.

March 12

MANCHESTER UNITED 2
QPR 0
(Half-time score : 1-0)

United: Schmeichel, G Neville, Irwin, Bruce, Sharpe, Pallister, Kanchelskis, Ince, McClair, Hughes, Giggs (Keane 45).
Subs: P Neville, Walsh.
QPR: Roberts, Maddix, Wilson, Barker, Bardsley, Brevett (Penrice 61), Gallen, McDonald, Impey, Holloway, Ferdinand.
Scorers: Sharpe 22, Irwin 53.
Referee: D J Gallagher (Banbury).
Attendance: 42,830

Alex Ferguson watched Manchester United stride a step closer to an historic successive FA Cup and League Double and then made it clear he was staying as manager for the foreseeable future.

Fergie fuelled speculation about his eventual move to the United board even though he has two years left on his current contract. But he emphasised he had more footballing honours in his sights before the switch upstairs. "I have not achieved all I want to," he said. "Can you imagine me retiring? We have to move forward and keep striving for success."

At the same time he paid generous tribute to the work of his assistant Brian Kidd and made it plain he was his choice as successor. "If Kidd wants my job eventually, he will get it," said Ferguson.

Kidd, goal-scoring hero for United in the victorious 1968 European Cup final, has worked his way up from the rank of United youth development officer to be Fergie's right-hand man.

"Brian has done a magnificent job in all his roles here," said Ferguson. "Everyone at the club knows the work he has done and how instrumental he has been in all the success. He will have a vital say in the future running of this club."

United kept on course for the country's first back-to-back Double as goals from Lee Sharpe and Denis Irwin set them up for a semi-final against Crystal Palace or Wolves.

It was not United's most polished performance but even on an off-day they remain way above average. Rangers worked hard at stopping them from playing but had little confidence in their own ability to inflict damage on Peter Schmeichel's goal.

United have never lost to QPR in an FA Cup tie and there was no real danger of that record being disrupted, though the scuffle for midfield supremacy occasionally looked as if it should have been conducted with an oval ball.

Rangers' Ian Holloway, on his 32nd birthday, and Simon Barker slugged it out with Paul Ince, a robust contest which finished with honours even.

If there has been something lost in translation over recent disputes between Andrei Kanchelskis and the club, the Ukrainian was again speaking the language the fans love in this match. United are a better side when he is in the team and, although Sharpe was Fergie's man of the match, Rangers were damaged equally from both flanks.

The contest was at its most bruising through the middle, where Hughes was a tower of strength with his back to goal. Alan McDonald and Danny Maddix gave him their best shots but Hughes took it all with restraint until Maddix fouled him on the edge of the area. The two squared up like Las Vegas heavyweights and were lucky to remain on the pitch, since referee Dermot Gallagher had already booked both.

Instead the punishment came from the 53rd-minute free-kick because it produced the killer goal from Irwin's clubbing shot round the wall to make it 2-0.

By then United should have had the game wrapped up. Ryan Giggs, playing through the middle in the absence of the cup-tied Andy Cole, slid a Kanchelskis centre wide of an upright and Sharpe burst into the penalty area only to have Tony Roberts save with his legs.

The lead came in the 22nd minute from a build-up typical of United. Hughes again held up the ball under pressure before squaring it to Giggs. He spotted Sharpe moving into the box, released the ball and, as David Bardsley missed with a hasty challenge, the trusty left foot did the rest inside the far post.

Rangers attacked desperately in the closing stages. Rufus Brevett saw a good chance dribble past a post and McDonald failed with a header from five yards. Schmeichel added saves from Gary Penrice and Les Ferdinand.

Denis Irwin slams home United's second.

March 15

MANCHESTER UNITED 0
TOTTENHAM HOTSPUR 0
(Half-time score : 0-0)

United: Schmeichel, Cole, Irwin, Bruce, Sharpe, Pallister, Kanchelskis, Ince, McClair (Butt 76), Hughes, Giggs.
Subs: Walsh, Neville.
Tottenham: Walker, Austin, Edinburgh, Howells, Calderwood, Mabbutt, Barmby, Klinsmann, Anderton, Sheringham, Rosenthal.
Referee: K. Morton (Bury St Edmunds)
Attendance: 43,802.

League Table After Match

	P	W	D	L	F	A	Pts
Blackburn	34	23	7	4	70	29	76
Man Utd	33	21	7	5	63	22	70
Newcastle	32	17	9	6	54	33	60
Nottm Forrest	34	16	9	9	53	38	57
Liverpool	30	15	9	6	52	26	54
Leeds	32	14	10	8	44	30	52
Tottenham	32	14	9	9	52	42	51
Wimbledon	33	13	6	14	39	54	45
Sheff Wed	35	11	10	14	43	46	43
Coventry	35	10	13	12	37	53	43
QPR	31	11	8	12	49	50	41
Man City	33	10	11	12	43	50	41
Arsenal	32	10	10	12	36	36	40
Chelsea	32	10	10	12	40	45	40
Aston Villa	34	9	12	13	46	48	39
Norwich	33	9	12	12	30	38	39
Everton	34	9	12	13	37	46	39
West Ham	34	10	7	17	33	44	37
C Palace	32	8	10	14	23	34	34
Southampton	31	6	15	10	41	50	33
Ipswich	32	6	5	21	31	72	23
Leicester	34	4	9	21	36	66	21

It has been billed as the dream FA Cup final and Wembley is in for a real classic if United and Spurs do meet again under the twin towers. This scintillating match had everything: the style, swagger and sweat expected of great teams. Everything but the goals.

United's fans may worry that failure to win – they failed to score for the first time at Old Trafford this season – will unhinge their title challenge. Manager Alex Ferguson had warned that only victory would be good enough and his expensive side did not oblige. But the overwhelming feeling should have been a sense of privilege at witnessing a wonderful contest.

In the first half United pulverised Spurs from the kick-off, playing with a pace and passion which would have swept away lesser sides. Mark Hughes hit the post with a header inside 30 seconds and Andy Cole scooped an effort against the bar from six yards. Tottenham goalkeeper Ian Walker earned his reprieves with a series of outstanding saves to deny Paul Ince (twice), Ryan Giggs, Andrei Kanchelskis and Cole again, a fierce shot which ricocheted off the keeper's chest.

Kanchelskis treated the right wing as a personal Formula One racetrack. Giggs was equally effective along the left with his more jinking approach.

Everyone in the 43,000 crowd thought a goal had to come, surely from United, but half-time brought an amazing transformation. In the second half it was the turn of Tottenham, inspired by Jurgen Klinsmann, to show why, under the management of Gerry Francis, they have become one of the finest teams in the land.

They had defended with composure and showed a similar cool nerve in taking the game to United as Old Trafford suddenly grew anxious. Klinsmann's record of never scoring against Peter Schmeichel remained intact but only just. He lobbed one shot on to the roof of the net, then became provider with a flurry of finely judged passes to set up team-mates.

Ronny Rosenthal wasted a chance by running the ball too close to Schmeichel and Nick Barmby's cheeky chip moments later flew wide. Klinsmann also laid on Darren Anderton for a fierce drive blocked by the United goalkeeper.

By the finish a win for either side would have been hugely unjust. But in the last minute Rosenthal had to kick a shot from Giggs off the line with Walker beaten.

"We always seem to make life difficult for ourselves," said Ferguson. "We could have been two or three up and then frittered away the second half. We were brilliant in the first half and I can't believe a game like that has finished 0-0. But Spurs are tough and resilient and they made it hard for us.

It's the last four or five games that really count and when mistakes tell. The championship could go down to the wire."

Foiled again. . .
Spurs keep
out Paul Ince.

March 19

LIVERPOOL 2

MANCHESTER UNITED 0

(Half-time score : 1-0)

Liverpool: James, Wright, Babb, Ruddock, Scales, McManaman, Barnes (Thomas 61), Redknapp, Bjornebye, Fowler, Rush (Walters 88).
United: Schmeichel, Irwin, Bruce, Sharpe (Cole 45), Pallister, Ince, McClair, Keane (Butt 83), Kanchelskis, Hughes, Giggs.
Sub: Pilkington.
Scorers: Redknapp 25, Bruce 85 og.
Referee: G R Ashby (Worcester).
Attendance: 38,906

An inspirational display by Jamie Redknapp helped Liverpool inflict a massive blow to United's title ambitions.

Redknapp, at 21 the rising midfield star in English soccer, was signed by Kenny Dalglish shortly before the Scot's Anfield departure four years ago. Here he scored a brilliant goal and laboured mightily in midfield to push Dalglish, his lifetime idol, closer to a championship triumph with Blackburn.

As referee Gerald Ashby sounded the final whistle to end this tribal battle the Anfield faithful joyously chanted "Dalglish". It was the fans' affectionate way of proclaiming their belief that the past weekend may prove a watershed in the title struggle.

To Alex Ferguson they sent a less warm message. "You've lost the League on Merseyside," they told the United manager.

The bookies are veering away from United, with Blackburn now 13-8 on to land the crown and Ferguson's side 5-4. Blackburn have to visit Merseyside, to face Everton on April 1, and are due at Anfield for the final league game of the season on May 14.

Dalglish's old club could not have given more to halt United and leave them six points adrift of Blackburn. Defeat was painful enough for Alex Ferguson's side but the knife was twisted by a booking for Steve Bruce which rules the United captain out of four games including the FA Cup semi-final and the home duel with Leeds.

His yellow card for cynically ending a Redknapp run took him over 41 disciplinary points, into a third ban this season and a date with the FA Disciplinary Commission. Bruce's afternoon of agony was completed five minutes from the end when his own goal secured the Liverpool triumph.

The Anfield team's demolition of the ragged champions was achieved through a superb team performance. Part of the reason was the return after thigh damage of John Barnes who made a telling contribution for an hour before having to make way for Michael Thomas.

If England Under-21 skipper Redknapp rightly earned commendation for his blend of sweat and skill, comeback veteran Mark Wright also won combat honours. With Rob Jones suspended, manager Roy Evans plunged 31-year-old Wright into his first senior outing for a year and switched John Scales to full-back.

The former England centre-back Wright had been axed from the squad by Evans last summer and subsequently ruled out with calf and Achilles problems. But he responded in stirring style to being pitched into a contest played in a frenzied atmosphere.

United provided the first shock when the team sheet showed £7 million striker Andy Cole on the bench. Ferguson explained later that he had suffered a thigh strain in training the previous day. Cole was sent on at the start of the second half as United withdrew Lee Sharpe, hoping to give lone attacker Mark Hughes much needed support. But Cole never got a sniff.

Liverpool forged ahead after 25 minutes with a that goal started and magnificently finished by Redknapp. He found Barnes who, despite falling, took possession off Gary Pallister and passed to Robbie Fowler.

The 19-year-old steered the ball into Redknapp's path on the left and he side-stepped Denis Irwin to fire a left-foot shot past Peter Schmeichel low into the far corner of the net. It was his fifth goal of the season and his first in the Premiership at home.

Redknapp almost created a second six minutes later when his pin-point-pass sent Fowler through only for the England B raider to be denied by Schmeichel's fingertips. United's shooting, such as it was, was wayward with David James having only two saves to make, from Hughes and the disappointing Ryan Giggs.

United's second defeat in 19 games, following their 1-0 reverse at Everton last month, was assured five minutes from the end. Thomas, a lively substitute, crossed from the right and when Steve McManaman connected the ball struck Bruce and flew past the wrong-footed Schmeichel.

League Table After Match

	P	W	D	L	F	A	Pts
Blackburn	34	23	7	4	70	29	76
Man Utd	34	21	7	6	63	24	70
Newcastle	33	18	9	6	55	33	63
Liverpool	31	16	9	6	54	26	57
Nottm Forest	34	16	9	9	53	38	57
Leeds	32	14	10	8	44	30	52
Tottenham	32	14	9	9	52	42	51
Wimbledon	33	13	6	14	39	54	45
Sheff Wed	35	11	10	14	43	46	43
Coventry	35	10	13	12	37	53	43
QPR	31	11	8	12	49	50	41
Man City	33	10	11	12	43	50	41
Arsenal	33	10	10	13	36	37	40
Chelsea	32	10	10	12	40	45	40
Aston Villa	34	9	12	13	46	48	39
Norwich	33	9	12	12	43	38	39
Everton	34	9	12	13	37	46	39
West Ham	34	10	7	17	33	44	37
C Palace	32	8	10	14	23	34	34
Southampton	31	6	15	10	41	50	33
Ipswich	32	6	5	21	31	72	23
Leicester	34	4	9	23	36	66	21

March 22

MANCHESTER UNITED 3

ARSENAL 0

(Half-time score : 2-0)

United: Schmeichel, Irwin, Bruce, Sharpe, Pallister, Ince, Hughes, Giggs, Kanchelskis, Keane, Cole.
Subs: McClair, Butt, Pilkington.
Arsenal: Bartram, Dixon, Winterburn, Adams, Wright, Merson, Bould, Keown, Morrow, Parlour (Helder 57), Kiwomya.
Scorers: Hughes 26, Sharpe 31, Kanchelskis 80.
Referee: K Cooper (Pontypridd).
Attendance: 43,623.

Ian Wright clashed with Steve Bruce in an amazing half-time bust-up at Old Trafford as football's season of sleaze continued. The controversial Arsenal striker squared up to the Manchester United skipper as the pair trooped up the tunnel.

Eyewitnesses claimed Wright, still seething at his 42nd-minute booking for a foul on Bruce, turned on the centre-half. Bruce did not retaliate and security guards and police dived in to break up the melee.

The Arsenal striker, already suspended three times this season for amassing 41 disciplinary points, was visibly furious at the booking. He angrily gestured at Bruce as referee Keith Cooper brandished the yellow card. Bruce, who this week became only the third player in England to reach 41 points, was himself booked in the second half for fouling Wright.

A United spokesman insisted: "It was a minor incident that blew over very quickly. These incidents are not unknown in the tunnel area."

Anything less than victory against Arsenal and United would have been condemned men in the great championship trial of strength. But an inspirational performance from their midfield dynamo Paul Ince and goals from Mark Hughes, Lee Sharpe and Andrei Kanchelskis ensured the jury stays out on their title tussle with Blackburn.

For Arsenal, though, this was their fourth Premiership defeat on the trot and, if relegation is not an immediate threat, the danger looms large enough.

This was a match United could not afford to lose and manager Alex Ferguson, on the eve of his trip to Buckingham Palace to collect his CBE, threw down a challenge to his side by questioning their hunger for more honours.

His fears, articulated in some blunt programme notes, produced the sort of response he expected as United set about the visitors with the kind of panache that has deservedly brought them consecutive championships.

Afterwards the United boss claimed: "Asking whether the players had the hunger was a question that had to be put. We have not come back in any game this season whereas last time we rescued two or three from nothing.

"Every game from now until the end of the season will be like this one because we simply have to win them. You can get used to success and forget how you earned it in the first place.

"But if we keep this up we can get back into things. The team responded well and everyone raised their game."

United's previous two games had yielded one point and no goals, and Arsenal, with a midfield of Martin Keown and Steve Morrow clearly intent on containment, came with the intention of reducing United to another frustrating 90 minutes.

But their intention to throttle the game looked doomed to failure after only four minutes when Sharpe flashed a 20-yard shot narrowly wide. Then the familiar figure of Hughes popped up with another vital goal to add to the many he has claimed in his United career.

Stand-in goalkeeper Vince Bartram could only get his fingertips to a Ryan Giggs cross and, when Sharpe's shot fell to Hughes, he rifled it home gleefully.

All the tension evaporated from United's play and it was no surprise when they went two ahead five minutes later, Hughes and Kanchelskis combining to set up Sharpe for a low right-foot drive.

Arsenal were forced to rely on counter-attack and although Wright narrowly missed a contender for goal of the season when his 50-yard lob flew over Peter Schmeichel but just wide, it was in a more familiar role that the axed England striker made his mark. He clattered into Bruce shortly before the break to pick up yet another booking and was joined in the notebook by Keown and Bruce, the latter for repaying the favour on the Arsenal striker.

Arsenal, despite their precarious league position, looked content merely to avoid another Ipswich-style drubbing from United rather than claw back a precious point and it was no surprise when Kanchelskis stretched the lead after 79 minutes.

United's top scorer tucked the ball home from a tight angle after Bartram parried a Giggs shot.

The margin could easily have been stretched by Andy Cole but the

League Table After Match

	P	W	D	L	F	A	Pts
Blackburn	34	23	7	4	70	29	76
Man Utd	35	22	7	6	66	24	73
Newcastle	34	18	9	7	56	36	63
Nottm Forest	35	17	9	9	56	38	60
Liverpool	32	16	10	6	54	26	58
Leeds	33	14	10	9	44	33	52
Tottenham	33	14	10	9	52	42	52
Wimbledon	34	14	6	14	41	54	48
QPR	32	12	8	12	50	50	44
Sheff Wed	35	11	10	14	43	46	43
Coventry	35	10	13	12	37	53	43
Norwich	34	10	12	12	33	38	42
Man City	34	10	11	13	43	52	41
Arsenal	34	10	10	14	36	40	40
Chelsea	33	10	10	13	40	46	40
Aston Villa	34	9	12	13	46	48	39
Everton	34	9	12	13	37	46	39
West Ham	34	10	7	17	33	44	37
Southampton	32	7	15	10	44	51	36
C Palace	32	8	10	14	23	34	34
Ipswich	33	6	5	22	31	75	23
Leicester	34	4	9	21	36	66	21

£7 million man continued to show a remarkable inconsistency in front of goal. His five-goal haul against Ipswich was a distant memory as he scooped over the bar from less than five yards and then failed to control an Ince cross.

Arsenal boss Stewart Houston claimed: "There are eight games left and plenty of points to play for and it is up to us to make sure we remain in the Premiership next year.

"We were solid early on but goals change games. When they got their second within five minutes of the first the whole complexion of the match was different.

"It was important for us to make a good start and, although we did that, it was tough for us to come back at a place like Old Trafford."

Bruce and Wright clash . . . there was to be a re-match in the players' tunnel.

April 2

Eric Cantona can start writing another poem: a lament to Manchester United's title hopes.

The Frenchman revealed his nautical leanings during a court appearance last week, talking eloquently, if obscurely, about seagulls following boats. Now United's championship trawler is sinking fast.

Alex Ferguson thinks it is all over and the large contingent who filed out of Old Trafford five minutes before the final whistle were clearly in agreement. Blackburn can go eight points clear with victory against QPR but more important than the arithmetic according to Fergie are the omens.

And these certainly did not look to be behind United on a sunny afternoon when anything less than victory would surely seal the end of their dreams of a third successive title.

Whether the Old Trafford boss has broken a mirror or two is not known but he could have hoped for more luck in front of goal as United tore into Leeds. Chance after chance flashed past in a breathless second half but there always seemed to be something to stop the vital goal in the shape of the visitors' massed defence.

United have lost the goal touch at the crucial time, failing to score for the third time in four games, and even Andy Cole's best performance for the club was not enough.

With Andrei Kanchelskis injured, Fergie recalled David Beckham from his loan to Preston and the 20-year-old did not disappoint. Playing in an unfamiliar right-wing role, he set up the first chance of the game after 23 minutes when he crossed for Ryan Giggs at the far post. The Welsh winger caught the volley crisply but fired it straight at John Lukic in goal.

That was United's only real chance in a first half when endeavour was not matched by enterprise. Even Paul Ince could not find the spark to lift the game from its strangely subdued atmosphere.

But that all changed in the second half when the match caught fire and the fans had something better to do than taunt each other as they had non-stop throughout the first period. The visiting contingent took great delight in chants of "Dalglish". But if they were hoping to knock United off their stride, it seemed to have the reverse effect as the revi-

MANCHESTER UNITED 0
LEEDS 0
(Half-time score : 0-0)

United: Schmeichel, Irwin, Pallister, Ince, McClair, Hughes, Giggs, Keane, Cole, Neville, Beckham.
Subs: Scholes, Butt, Walsh.
Leeds: Lukic, Kelly, Dorigo, Palmer, Pemberton, Wetherall, Yeboah, Wallace (Worthington 87), Deane (Whelan 82), McAllister, Couzens.
Referee: R B Gifford (Llanbradach)
Attendance: 43,712

talised Reds launched a barrage of second-half attacks.

Cole, at last showing the linking play which had been sorely missing from his game, worked a wonderful move with Mark Hughes and, when he pulled the ball back for the on-rushing Brian McClair, a goal looked certain. But the Scottish midfielder pulled his 59th minute shot wide to cries of frustration from the Stretford end.

The England debutant was again heavily involved in the 73rd minute when Giggs was thwarted by the excellent David Wetherall, and Hughes failed to hit the target with the rebound.

Leeds, clearly content to play for the draw after their FA Cup humiliation at Old Trafford, still managed to carve out their own chances as United pressed forward for that much-needed goal.

Peter Schmeichel almost gifted them the lead three minutes after the interval when he lazily went to clear a back pass from Roy Keane, who was an admirable stand-in for suspended skipper Steve Bruce alongside Gary Pallister. The ball cannoned off the on-coming Carlton Palmer and only the massive back-spin on the ball prevented what would have been the worst clanger of the season.

Live-wire winger Rod Wallace also threatened several times but Leeds were more than content to sit back and soak up the pressure.

Keane pushed forward with 10 minutes left on the clock as United sank into desperation but, as Fergie feared, the omens were not with them.

The title race is by no means over but Fergie was right when he said it would take a Devon Loch by Blackburn to give them a glimmer of hope.

United's fate is well and truly out of their hands. Blackburn play three more Premiership matches before United resume their challenge against Leicester City in just under a fortnight. By then, their championship crown, already slipping, could be heading to Ewood Park and the head of king Kenny Dalglish.

"Blackburn can only throw the league away now," said Ferguson. "We can only hope they do a Devon Loch. It's going to take a real major boob by them. You can't mask this type of result at such an important stage of the season.

"We will continue to battle as we always do, but this was not so much a crucial result as a decisive one. It's very disappointing because I thought we played very well.

"We put them under a lot of pressure in the second half and the players can all put their hand on their heart and say they did not let anyone down. I was thinking about shaking it up in the second half but no one deserved to come off."

Ferguson revealed that Kanchelskis missed the game after having eight pain-killing injections before his midweek appearance for Russia against Scotland. He is furious that the Russians approved the injections to allow Kanchelskis to get through 90 minutes and United intend to take up the matter with their FA.

Ferguson said: "Andrei had the injections for his stomach trouble and I am angry. We have never given a player a pain-killing injection to get through the game. And we will certainly be pursuing the matter.

"It is all very strange. We have put him in for scans but no one has been able to find anything wrong with him. He feels there is a pain there and the Russians decided they should give him this treatment."

League Table After Match

	P	W	D	L	F	A	Pts
Blackburn	36	25	7	4	73	30	82
Man Utd	36	22	8	6	66	24	74
Newcastle	36	19	10	7	60	37	67
Nottm Forest	37	18	10	9	64	40	64
Liverpool	34	17	10	7	57	28	61
Leeds	36	16	11	9	49	33	59
Tottenham	34	14	10	10	55	46	52
Wimbledon	35	15	6	14	45	57	51
QPR	35	14	8	13	54	52	50
Sheff Wed	37	12	10	15	45	53	46
Aston Villa	36	10	13	13	47	48	43
Arsenal	36	11	10	15	42	44	43
Coventry	36	10	13	13	37	54	43
Norwich	37	10	12	15	34	47	42
Chelsea	34	10	11	13	41	47	41
Man City	35	10	11	14	44	54	41
Southampton	34	8	15	11	49	57	39
Everton	35	9	12	14	38	48	39
C Palace	34	9	11	14	25	35	38
West Ham	35	10	8	17	34	45	38
Leicester	37	5	9	23	40	71	24
Ipswich	35	6	5	24	31	80	23

Andy Cole is stopped on the way to a goal.

April 9

MANCHESTER UNITED 2
CRYSTAL PALACE 2

*(Half-time score : 0-1
after extra time)*

United: Schmeichel, Irwin, Pallister, Neville, Ince, Sharpe, Keane, McClair, Beckham (Butt 49), Hughes, Giggs.
Subs: Scholes, Walsh.
Palace: Martyn, Patterson, Coleman (Gordon 46), Young, Shaw, Pitcher, Southgate, Houghton, Armstrong, Dowie, Salako.
Scorers: (United): Irwin 70, Pallister 96; (Crystal Palace): Dowie 33, Armstrong 92
Referee: D Elleray (Middlesex)
Attendance: 38,256

Gary Pallister called it the most important goal of his life and none of the United faithful at Villa Park were arguing after the big defender's extra-time header kept alive their hopes of back-to-back FA Cup successes.

United had to come from behind twice in a thriller and Pallister said: "It's only my third of the season. I don't score many but that has to be the most important of my career. I was delighted with it because it has kept us in the competition."

Heroic goalkeeper Nigel Martyn kept Palace's Wembley dream alive after battling through 120 minutes with a suspected broken hand. But Palace's hopes of a replay victory were rocked by Martyn's injury, suffered in a clash with David Beckham in the second minute.

Martyn, who went straight to hospital for X-rays on his badly swollen hand, said: "I could hardly feel my hand throughout the whole game. It's still very sore. There's not a lot of time between now and Wednesday but I badly want to play because I feel a bit responsible for their second goal, which let them back into the game."

It was a dramatic and unpredictable roller-coaster of a match and Palace boss Alan Smith said: "They didn't have many chances apart from the two goals but they are so outstanding you can never relax. We will just have to make sure we get back to London and get fit for the replay."

Pugnacious Iain Dowie, a cut-price striker bought to help Palace in their relegation battle, and Chris Armstrong, still living down a drugs scandal, were nearly the match-winning heroes. But first Denis Irwin and then Pallister rescued United and ruined what would have been a glorious afternoon for the underdog.

Everton had ripped up the ticket for the Wembley dream final by defeating Tottenham earlier in the afternoon and Palace emerged with nightmarish intent against United.

With title ambitions slipping away to Blackburn, United's bid to retain this half of their 1994 Double – and in the process reach a record 13th Cup final took on extra urgency.

Palace had the appearance of a club in turmoil on their arrival in the Midlands. Premiership survival was their priority, and a feud between manager Smith and chairman and owner Ron Noades was an obvious distraction.

There was no disharmony on the field, though, as they defied the odds and gave impressive backing to Smith – as did their supporters vocally – in adding to United's uncertain and troubled recent experiences. Palace ruthlessly tore up the form book and for large periods of this tense encounter took the devil out of United, who were admittedly without their inspirational skipper Steve Bruce, the Cup-tied striker Andy Cole and the banned Eric Cantona.

There were indications of the drama to follow in the early stages as Palace, superbly organised, blunted United's attempts at their usual style and invention. More significantly, the handling of goalkeeper Peter Schmeichel looked far from convincing.

The big Danish keeper played a part in Palace's opening goal after 33 minutes. He pawed out a cross from John Salako and Armstrong cut the ball back over his head into the goalmouth. Salako this time used his head to put it back across the six-yard box and Dowie, with a dip of the head, scored a goal which looked like repaying all of the £400,000 he cost from Southampton.

A minute later United's plight could have been deepened when the impressive Gareth Southgate sent Armstrong scurrying clear but his shot, while wide of Schmeichel, also went the wrong side of the upright.

United boss Alex Ferguson had by this time dashed down to the bench, aware of an impending crisis, with even Pallister showing signs of panic in collecting his first booking of the season. Whatever an obviously irate Ferguson said in the dressing room at half-time, it revitalised United.

But for all their renewed endeavour they still looked suspect in the early minutes of the second half. Dowie was presented with a great opportunity to produce another goal-bound header. Again it stemmed from an error by Schmeichel, who kicked the ball out directly to Ray Houghton, but his cross was put wide by the Northern Ireland international.

United restored their dignity with a 70th-minute equaliser from unsung hero Irwin. He conjured up a spectacular free-kick from just outside the penalty box, curling the ball into the top corner.

Any thoughts that the tide had now turned were dismissed when Armstrong went clear again only to screw the ball wide.

Houghton, 33 and playing in only his third game since his deadline signing from Aston Villa, seemed to gain inspiration as 90 minutes passed and the game went into added time, while United must have looked at the extra 30 minutes with foreboding.

Five years earlier Palace had confounded the pundits with an extra-time victory over a Liverpool side containing Houghton and memories of that surged back when, within 63 seconds of the restart, Armstrong restored Palace's lead. Southgate clipped the ball through and Armstrong, while seeming to misjudge his lob, nevertheless steered it over the head of Schmeichel.

That was Armstrong's tenth goal in cup competitions this season but United's equaliser came within four minutes when Pallister strode forward to meet a Gary Neville throw and flick the ball into the far corner of the Palace net.

It was the last act of the day because although United, served brilliantly again by Mark Hughes, strove for a winner Palace, were in no mood to concede anything.

Now the sides return to Villa Park on Wednesday evening to renew their struggle, with Palace uncomfortably aware that United proved the victors in a replay in the 1990 final.

Ferguson said: "Palace always take us to the edge. It must have been an exciting game to watch."

April 12

Roy Keane and Darren Patterson were sent off in disgrace as the so-called FA Cup semi-final of peace erupted in violence. The double dismissal and mass mêlée, three days after a supporter was killed in a fight between United and Palace fans, made a mockery of the pleas before this replay for harmony.

Both managers had made an unprecedented call for calm from the Villa Park centre circle 10 minutes before kick-off. But that was soon forgotten as Keane was dismissed for a stamp and Patterson followed for retaliating angrily as both sides dived into the second half fracas.

United skipper Steve Bruce, who put United on course for another Wembley appearance, conceded: "The fans have behaved themselves. But it is time we got our whole house in order and went back to how we were a few months ago."

Keane became United's fifth dismissal of the season but Alex Ferguson refused to go overboard in his condemnation of the Irishman's wild loss of discipline. He said: "It's incredible that this has happened, tonight of all nights. Roy deserved to be sent off, you can't agree with what he did. It was silly and you can't excuse it. But we will handle it as we always do without broadcasting it to the world. "There's a lot of tension about and we were hoping that nothing would happen. Roy was about to come off because he had seven stitches in his ankle at half-time but then it all happened."

Patterson, who reacted furiously after Keane stamped on skipper Gareth Southgate following a wild tackle by the Palace player, said: "Why did I go in there? I should have left him alone." Five other players were cautioned by Harrow referee David Elleray for shows of pettiness or ill-temper.

Only 17,987 fans turned up – the lowest ever recorded for an FA Cup semi-final – to observe a minute's silence for the dead fan Paul Nixon and the players wore arm bands in honour of the Palace supporter.

The record book will not show what a poor game this was, only that it carried United to an unprecedented 13th final appearance with the chance of a record ninth win. On each of their last four visits to Wembley they have needed a semi-final replay to get there. But, as

MANCHESTER UNITED 2

CRYSTAL PALACE 0

(Half-time score : 2-0)

United: Schmeichel, Neville, Irwin, Bruce, Sharpe, Pallister, Butt, Ince, Keane, Hughes, Giggs (McClair59).
Subs: Scholes, Walsh
Palace: Wilmot, Patterson, Gordon, Southgate, Young, Shaw, Pitcher, (Newman 81), Dowie (Cox 81), Armstrong, Houghton, Salako
Scorers: Bruce, 30, Pallister, 41
Referee: D Elleray (Harrow)
Attendance: 17,987

Villa Park staged its 46th semi, United had the reassuring statistic of not having lost at the ground in five previous visits. There was never much danger of them losing this game, even without Cantona, Andy Cole and Andrei Kanchelskis.

The match swung on two thudding headers from the central defenders Bruce and Gary Pallister. Fortified by the return of Bruce and with the youthful and zealous Nicky Butt and the plundering Paul Ince in midfield, United always carried too much ammunition. Palace were outgunned by the heavy weaponry rather than played off the pitch by customary United style. Palace fans who boycotted the game and turned their satellite dishes towards the Midlands were fearful that Rhys Wilmot's rustiness might be the decisive factor in the game. But the 33-year-old goalkeeper, who had not played a senior football match for 23 months, could not be faulted as he stood in the face of Ince's howitzers without flinching.

His confidence was settled by a second-minute save from Butt and in an opening 20 minutes of United domination he was hardly allowed time to think about his ordeal. Palace, after their aggressive and confident football in the first game, seldom looked threatening though Pallister became the first player booked when he obstructed Chris Armstrong on the break. Occasionally there were glimpses of United's pedigree – a flashing header from Ince and a volley from Ryan Giggs – but it was Bruce who opened the scoring.

When Lee Sharpe looped over a corner in the 29th minute, Bruce's intended marker Ian Dowie was on the touchline having a contact lens replaced leaving the United skipper the chance of a soaring header. Five minutes from half-time Bruce's partner Pallister delivered the last rites on Palace's Cup ambitions with another towering header, from Sharp's free-kick.

Palace's efforts to raise their game in the second half found Bruce in unrivalled form. But the abiding memory of the half will remain the sight of players running towards the scene of Keane's fracas, another unseemly sight for a game already sadly scarred. Punishment for Keane should be serious from his club, if not from the Football Association, as this was the conduct of a rowdy delinquent. Perhaps

Fergie will omit him from the final which, it must be hoped, will offer the more acceptable face of the game.

The last time Everton beat Manchester United in an FA Cup game was at Old Trafford in 1969. The scorer was Joe Royle.

Patterson getting sent off.

April 15

MANCHESTER UNITED 4

LEICESTER 0

(Half-time score : 2-0)

United: Schmeichel, Irwin, Bruce, Sharpe (Beckham 46), Pallister, Ince, McClair, Hughes (Scholes 55), Cole, Butt, Neville.
Sub: Walsh.
Leicester: Poole, Grayson (Blake 55), Whitlow, Willis, Hill, Draper, Parker, Lawrence, Roberts, Robins, Lowe (Carey 74).
Scorers: Sharpe 33, Cole 45, 52, Ince 90,
Referee: M Bodenham (East Looe).
Attendance: 21,281

The title is not conceded yet. Alex Ferguson can drive players to do anything, as the Scottish player who sat in the dressing room, frightened to death, with a pair of underpants on his head was ready to testify.

Mark McGhee recalled the occasion after his relegated Leicester team had been thrashed by a Manchester United side supposedly on the Championship ropes.

McGhee played for Ferguson when he managed Aberdeen and dominated Scottish football. They had regular dressing-room bust-ups and, although McGhee says that the maths dictate the title is likely go to Ewood Park, he does not underestimate how fiery Fergie can influence players.

"Me and Alex had a very volatile dressing-room relationship," says McGhee. " Were teacups flying? Aye, and the pies, but there is one occasion that illustrates just how much Fergie can strike the fear of God into his players.

"We were playing a game at Forfar in the Aberdeenshire Senior Cup and Fergie's No2, Archie Knox, had come into the dressing-room and was tearing into the team.

" Behind him came Fergie and he started shouting and yelling at this centre-forward called Stevie Cowan. As Fergie walked forward he kicked the dirty pile of kit and washing on the floor all over the place and a pair of underpants floated through the air and landed on the head of the boy sitting next to Cowan.

"While Cowan was getting slaughtered, the boy next to him didn't move. He was rigid with fear, sitting there bolt upright with these underpants on his head." Alex finished slaughtering Cowan and then barked at the other lad: 'And you, get those ------- pants off your head!'"

Although Ferguson now likes to portray a smiling image, McGhee suspects nothing has changed.

"Alex is a great psychologist too," says McGhee. " I'd be wanting to bound into the dressing room at half-time thinking what a good game I'd had, and Fergie would lay into me. He'd get me so mad I'd go out and have a blinder again and then on the way home I'd be thinking:

'The bugger, he's wound me up and got just what he wanted from me!'"

Fergie's words to his team before going out to meet Leicester were: "Relax, just play the way you want to play and sod the rest." And that is what they did. There was no controversy and no doubt what the result was going to be – just how many.

After they had gone three up early in the second half United seemed to call it a day, playing out time until they heard the final score from Blackburn's game at Elland Road.

Ferguson, by his own admission , sat content on the bench, enjoying what he was seeing and comforting himself with the thought that, if Blackburn do slip-up in their last five games, then United are there to snatch the prize from them.'

"That's the way it has to be," said United captain Steve Bruce. If they slip we have to be in position ready to pounce. That's what this victory was about."

Bruce is even ready to hand over the goal he scored to Andy Cole if he wants to claim it. "Cole is the £7 million striker," says Bruce. "If he wants it, he can have it because the pressure is on him to get goals, not me."

The Eric Cantona affair, the death of a Crystal Palace fan, Roy Keane's sending-off: all these incidents are being used by United to feed off. They are closing ranks, believing the world and its dog are against them, and out of it there has come a reinforced team spirit that Blackburn, even at this late stage, have to be careful of.

"We are keeping the pressure up and we are going to bust a gut to try and win this Championship," says Bruce. "Some of our football against Leicester was magnificent. We have had a tough time with everything that has gone on at this club but one thing I have learned about this lot in my time at United is the resilience and the character of the club.

"They will not buckle here. We get more knocks than anybody else in football but we will not cave in. There is a fierce determination to pull it off and win the league again." Fergie would be proud of that rallying call.

League Table After Match

	P	W	D	L	F	A	Pts
Blackburn	37	25	8	4	74	31	83
Man Utd	37	23	8	6	70	24	77
Nottm Forrest	38	19	10	9	65	40	67
Newcastle	37	19	10	8	60	39	67
Liverpool	36	18	10	8	59	30	64
Leeds	37	16	12	9	50	34	60
Tottenham	36	15	11	10	58	48	56
QPR	37	15	8	14	56	54	53
Wimbledon	37	15	7	15	46	61	52
Arsenal	38	12	10	16	46	46	46
Sheff Wed	38	12	10	16	45	55	46
Coventry	37	11	13	13	39	54	46
Southampton	36	10	15	11	53	58	45
Chelsea	37	11	12	14	43	50	45
Man City	37	11	11	15	47	54	44
Aston Villa	37	10	13	14	47	49	43
Everton	36	10	12	14	40	48	42
Norwich	36	10	12	16	34	48	42
West Ham	36	11	8	17	37	45	41
C Palace	35	9	12	14	26	36	39
Leicester	38	5	9	24	40	75	24
Ipswich	37	6	5	26	32	85	23

Bruce and the other senior professionals like Paul Ince, Gary Pallister, Mark Hughes and Brian McClair will be asked to lead by example again today against Chelsea, because all around them will be kids. Keane, Ryan Giggs and Andrei Kanchelskis are out injured and it will be the youth of Nicky Butt, Gary Neville, Paul Scholes and David Beckham who will be asked to continue to take the fight to Blackburn.

Sharpe, Ince and Cole (twice) scored the goals that United decided they would help themselves against Leicester and, if there is a criticism, it is that United and, in particular, Cole were wasteful. But when there are so many riches, why worry about forgetting to pick up one or two?

"If these players can continue winning," says Ferguson. "Who knows? This could be the biggest triumph in the history of the club. When Blackburn were one up at Leeds, I thought what a good result that would be for them to win there. But if mistakes are starting to be made, then who knows?" And it has McGhee wondering. Is Fergie at it, spreading a little doubt into a few minds at Blackburn? We have five more games to find out.

Schmeichel punches the ball clear.

April 17

Alex Ferguson's hold on the Premiership trophy was loosened by a Chelsea side who stoically drew up their battle lines and invited United to find a weakness in their defence. And, just as they had failed against Leeds earlier in the month, so United found themselves misusing their opportunities.

It was a tactical triumph for the Chelsea manager Glen Hoddle who used the knowledge that United were without their wing threat to fortify the centre of his defence. By employing Nigel Spackman and David Lee defensively in front of Frank Sinclair and Erland Johnsen, Chelsea effectively sealed the main route United had into the Chelsea penalty area.

It was Chelsea, of course, who threatened to spoil United's party last season, when they were the only side to complete the double over the champions. This time they treated the Theatre of Dreams like their own back yard. United tried all they could, sending Denis Irwin on exhausting runs down the left flank on an increasingly soggy pitch. On the other flank United used first David Beckham, then Simon Davies and ultimately Brian McClair but none could make up for the loss of Lee Sharpe, Ryan Giggs and Andrei Kanchelskis. It was this inability to get the ball behind the Chelsea full-backs Steve Clarke and Gareth Hall which led to the increasing frustration that swept through the packed terraces.

United have now drawn five out of 15 league games in 1995. In other words, they have dropped 10 points and their failure to capitalise on chances might be the difference between taking the prize and finishing second.

As they review another lost opportunity, they will examine two excellent chances in the first half. The first came in the fifth minute when Mark Hughes stole the ball from the toes of his own captain Steve Bruce but then saw it rebound off his shins and wide of Kevin Hitchcock's goal. The second fell to Nicky Butt, when Gary Neville offered him a free header in the 25th minute, but again the opening was squandered. Neville's service seemed the likeliest source of a breakthrough for the champions and he must have wondered what he had to do when McClair also headed over.

MANCHESTER UNITED 0
CHELSEA 0
(Half-time score : 0-0)

United: Schmeichel, Irwin, Bruce, Pallister, Ince, McClair, Hughes, Cole, Butt, Neville, Beckham (Davies 46).
Chelsea: Hitchcock, Clarke, Hall, Johnsen, Sinclair, Furlong (Spencer 67), Stein, Peacock, Spackman, Rocastle (Burley 59), Lee.
Referee: S J Lodge (Barnsley).
Attendance: 43,728.

League Table After Match

	P	W	D	L	F	A	Pts
Blackburn	38	25	8	5	76	34	83
Man Utd	38	23	9	6	70	24	78
Nottm Forrest	39	20	10	9	67	40	70
Liverpool	37	19	10	8	61	30	67
Newcastle	38	19	10	9	61	41	67
Leeds	38	17	12	9	52	35	63
Tottenham	37	16	11	10	59	48	59
QPR	38	15	8	15	56	55	53
Wimbledon	38	15	7	16	46	63	52
Arsenal	39	13	10	16	50	46	49
Southampton	37	11	15	11	55	58	48
Man City	38	12	11	15	50	59	47
Sheff Wed	39	12	11	16	45	55	47
Chelsea	38	11	13	14	43	50	46
Coventry	38	11	13	14	39	56	46
Aston Villa	38	10	13	15	47	53	43
Everton	37	10	13	14	40	48	43
West Ham	37	11	9	17	38	46	42
C Palace	36	10	12	14	27	36	42
Norwich	39	10	12	17	34	49	42
Leicester	39	5	9	25	40	77	24
Ipswich	38	6	6	26	33	86	24

Schmeicel
throws in the towel.

Andy Cole, who still to gets in to more goalscoring positions than most strikers, was in place when a lovely Hughes chip dropped invitingly but he lifted his shot over the bar. The traffic was relentlessly one way until the 32nd minute when a moment of carelessness allowed David Rocastle to present a chance to Gavin Peacock. Peacock scored the goals that beat United in the league last season and seemed likely to do so again until Schmeichel's agility and courage rescued the situation.

The second half followed a similar pattern and United were again denied a goal when Davies' cross was volleyed back from beyond the far post and Cole's header was somehow diverted for a corner by Sinclair.

A rare mistake by Bruce in the form of a bungled back-pass let in Mark Stein in the 71st minute but the little Chelsea striker lifted his shot over Schmeichel and the crossbar too.

Johnsen seemed to handle the ball 15 minutes from time from a long Neville throw-in – even Hoddle admitted it looked like a penalty and in the 89th minute Bruce, who had become the fourth man to operate the left flank, got in a cross which Scholes headed just over.

With that last chance, it seemed, United's title hopes had evaporated. United manager Alex Ferguson admitted: "If God is a Manchester United supporter he has got to act now. We are looking for miracles."

May 1

Those who scoffed at the £7m Alex Ferguson invested in Andy Cole were running for cover as the new dark destroyer of Old Trafford continued to repay his dues. Two goals of typical opportunism, making it 11 in 13 games since his move from Newcastle, continued the remarkable transformation in the Championship picture.

What might have been an 11-point lead for Blackburn Rovers is suddenly down to five and United still hold a game in hand against Sheffield Wednesday.

This contest, in which the Sky Blues of Coventry were seeking points to stay clear of the Premiership drop zone, had drama, excitement, pathos and a high level of skill .

The action now moves to Old Trafford on Sunday and who, after watching this, would not believe United are on a roll. They have watched Blackburn falter since January and they have fresh young legs as they canter for the finish line.

Here they were without five of their heavyweight stars Roy Keane and Paul Ince suspended, Steve Bruce, Andrei Kanchelskis and Ryan Giggs all injured.

Ferguson simply called into the nursery for Nicky Butt and Paul Scholes and pitched them into the mid-field to dispute the action with those wily old hands Gordon Strachan and Kevin Richardson.

Butt was outstanding and each time he wears the United red shirt he looks more and more like a footballer of genuine stature, an international in the making. Scholes, too, and this was a new role for him in midfield. Yet still he was the man who set United on the road to this success.

Spare a thought for Big Ron's side, however, for they contributed richly to a game that was as exciting as any Cup tie.

United were exhilarating and might have had the points wrapped up long before Cole's 79th-minute winner had it not been for the bravery and courage of Jonathan Gould. The son of ex-manager Bobby, stepping in after Steve Ogrizovic broke his leg the previous week, was peppered with buckshot in a relentless spell of United pressure in the first half and withstood it all.

The only sadness for Fergie on the night was an early booking for Gary Neville which could mean him missing the FA Cup final and leaving

---

COVENTRY 2
MANCHESTER UNITED 3
(Half-time score : 1-1)

Coventry: Gould, Hall, Rennie, Pressley, Borrows, Richardson, Strachan, Wegerle, Cook, Ndlovu, Dublin.
United: Schmeichel, Irwin, Sharpe, May, Pallister, Scholes (Beckham 76), McClair, Hughes, Cole, Butt, Neville.
Subs: McGibbon, Walsh,
Scorers: (Coventry): Ndlovu 39, Pressley 72; (United): Scholes 32, Cole 55, 79.
Referee: P Don (Middlesex).
Attendance: 21,885.

United a problem at right-back.

The scoring on this sticky night began in the 32nd minute as Cole stepped inside a defensive tackle on the right to send a piston of a shot at Gould. The goalkeeper did well to get down and block but he was unable to keep hold of the ball and, as it re-bounded, so Scholes thumped it back, first time, into the net.

It settled United and there was the old swagger to their play. They went for the throat and four times Gould cleared his six-yard area with flying fists.

Out of nowhere the blue sky opened up for the Sky Blues. A corner was poorly cleared and Dion Dublin performed a Cassius on his old club, driving the ball to the near post where Peter Ndlovu back-heeled it past Peter Schmeichel.

United had to start all over again. Gould denied Butt with a save from the gods but there was nothing he could do in the 55th minute when Butt's forward chip was missed by Steve Pressley. Cole was behind him in a flash, one on one with Gould and in those circumstances he rarely misses.

Pressley was all shook up, yet he atoned for his slip with an equaliser in the 72nd minute. Strachan, that distinguished United old boy, engineered the move, the excellent Paul Cook crossed and Pressley, with a free header, nodded home.

Again United needed to discover new resources only to find an unwitting ally in Richardson. He should have known better than to attempt a headed back-pass from 30 yards with Cole around. Cole intervened, hooked the ball over Gould's head and steered it home, a goal that might yet prove decisive as the season heads for its climax.

"They were the most important goals I have scored," said Cole. "I feel relaxed. For the first goal I just told myself to welly it because I've been trying to tap them in. I feel confident and, despite all the injuries we've had to important players, the squad is still big enough here to chase the title right to the death."

Ferguson said: "Now you see why I paid £7 million for Cole. It looks cheap when he gets important goals like that. When £3.7 million is paid for a centre-half, then how do you quibble about £7 million for a striker?"

League Table After Match

	P	W	D	L	F	A	Pts
Blackburn	40	26	8	6	78	37	86
Man Utd	39	24	9	6	73	26	81
Nottm Forrest	41	22	10	9	70	41	76
Liverpool	40	20	11	9	63	33	71
Newcastle	40	19	12	9	63	44	69
Leeds	40	19	12	9	55	36	69
Tottenham	40	16	13	11	64	54	61
QPR	41	16	9	16	58	57	57
Wimbledon	41	15	10	16	46	63	55
Southampton	40	12	17	11	58	59	53
Arsenal	41	13	12	16	51	47	51
Chelsea	41	12	15	14	48	54	51
Man City	41	12	13	16	51	61	49
Sheff Wed	40	12	12	16	45	55	48
Aston Villa	41	11	14	16	50	55	47
West Ham	40	12	10	18	40	47	46
Everton	40	10	16	14	43	51	46
Coventry	40	11	13	16	41	61	46
C Palace	40	11	12	17	31	53	45
Norwich	41	10	12	19	36	53	42
Leicester	41	6	10	25	43	78	28
Ipswich	40	7	6	27	35	88	27

May 7

David May, the defender who absconded from Blackburn Rovers and pitched tent at Old Trafford, scored the United goal that will test the fortitude of his old club. The gap which stood at eight points on April 2 has been whittled away to two and Blackburn's mettle will be put to the stress test when Newcastle visit Ewood Park in 24 hours' time.

The biggest crowd of the season, 43,868, had to endure 85 minutes of anxiety as United clung, precariously to May's fifth-minute strike.

For the devotees, watching United can be as fretful as standing outside a maternity ward waiting for the first-born and for much of this long afternoon a baby's whimper could easily have been heard. The silent vigil was an indication of how much tension is gripping these last stages of the title race. This was perhaps the most stuttering performance of the season from the champions, as starkly inarticulate as they had been fluent against Coventry a week ago.

These are testing days for Fergie's fledglings, boys sent out to perform jobs meant for men, and it is to their credit that they survived this ordeal without mishap.

The circumstances were not helped when May had to leave the stage after 24 minutes with a back injury, forcing young Gary Neville to move alongside Gary Pallister and accommodate his teenage brother Philip at right-back. It was a proud afternoon for Neville Neville, their father, who is secretary of Bury and who was in the stands to watch his sons. They both played with maturity beyond their years and Gary, especially, had an heroic game at the heart of the defence, confirming the belief that he is going to be a long-term asset to his club.

It was in mid-field that United wasted their opportunities, squandering possession and scattering passes.

Ferguson admitted he had probably selected wrongly by preferring Paul Scholes to Nicky Butt for it allowed the experienced John Sheridan too much sight of the ball.

Nor did Mark Hughes and Andy Cole seem as rapacious as usual though they found Des Walker in the kind of form that once made him the first name on England team sheets.

Wednesday defended stoutly but it is not difficult to see why they

MANCHESTER UNITED 1
SHEFFIELD WEDNESDAY 0
(Half-time score : 1-0)

United: Schmeichel, Irwin, Sharpe, Pallister, Ince, McClair, Hughes, May (P. Neville 24), Cole, Scholes (Butt 52), G. Neville.
Sub: Walsh.
Sheff Wed: Atherton, Nolan, Bright, Woods, Sheridan, Pearce, Bart-Williams, Hyde (Waddle 61), Walker, Whittingham (Poric 81), Williams.
Scorer: May 5
Referee: P A Durkin (Portland).
Attendance: 43, 868.

have won only one of their last nine games. Their forwards are clearly in crisis with the ball at their feet, so what was Chris Waddle doing on the bench?

United had every reason to be confident about the outcome before the game since they defeated Wednesday four times last season, twice in a two-leg League Cup tie and twice in the Premiership. And with Peter Schmeichel still to concede a goal in a league match at Old Trafford this season, everyone turned up for a Bank Holiday carnival.

It all started according to script with Chris Woods generating nostalgia with a lovely tip to keep out a typical cannon shot from Denis Irwin. From the corner Pallister headed back and there was May with a headed chance which Woods again got a hand to to touch on to the upright.

A minute later, however, May made amends as young Scholes turned the ball back from the byline. This time May's driven shot found the net despite Wednesday having players on the line.

The crowd sat back and waited for the avalanche. It never came. Instead they saw Hughes booked for exacting revenge on Sheridan and Lee Sharpe hit a half-volley wide from six yards.

Cole, who occasionally looked menacing, got his head to a Brian McClair cross and Woods again made the crucial save at the foot of his post.

When United did find momentum, so Walker raised his game and his clearance from Cole after Woods had blocked a shot from Butt was vintage defending.

League Table After Match

	P	W	D	L	F	A	Pts
Blackburn	40	26	8	6	78	37	86
Man Utd	40	25	9	6	74	26	84
Nottm Forrest	41	22	10	9	70	41	76
Liverpool	40	20	11	9	63	33	71
Newcastle	40	19	12	9	64	44	69
Leeds	40	19	12	9	55	36	69
Tottenham	40	16	13	11	64	54	61
QPR	41	16	9	16	58	57	57
Wimbledon	41	15	10	16	46	63	55
Southampton	40	12	17	11	58	59	53
Arsenal	41	13	12	16	51	47	51
Chelsea	41	12	15	14	48	54	51
Man City	41	12	13	16	51	61	49
Sheff Wed	41	12	12	17	45	56	48
Aston Villa	41	11	14	16	50	55	47
West Ham	40	12	10	18	40	47	46
Everton	40	10	16	14	43	51	46
Coventry	40	11	13	16	41	61	46
C Palace	40	11	12	17	31	43	45
Norwich	41	10	12	19	36	53	42
Leicester	41	6	10	25	43	78	28
Ipswich	40	7	6	27	35	88	27

May 10

Denis Irwin ripped the Premiership crown from the grasp of Kenny Dalglish with a controversial penalty. Just as the championship celebrations were about to start in Blackburn, Andy Cole went down under a challenge from Ken Monkou.

It may not have been a clear foul to most of the fans packed inside Old Trafford but referee Paul Danson had no doubts and that was good enough for them. He pointed straight to the spot to the fury of Alan Ball's men, who were still protesting long after the final whistle, and no doubt to the ire of the thousands who throng Ewood Park. But Irwin kept his cool to slot past David Beasant and set up a super last Sunday of this thrilling season.

For Cole it was a a night of special celebration. His first child was born 15 minutes before kick off, he breathed new life into the title race by firing United's equaliser and then he won the penalty.

After Blackburn's Victory at Ewood Day against Newcastle, this was Judgment Night at Old Trafford as United went in search of the victory that would keep their hopes alive.

The reappearance of Eric Cantona for the first time at a game since he began his lonely exile on that fateful night in January had already raised the roof. But it looked like becoming a nightmare after five minutes when Southampton took a lead that brought cheers to be heard within a 20 mile radius of Ewood Park.

Paul Charlton's strike blackened that particular surname for the first time in Old Trafford history and he became the first player to score there past Peter Schmeichel in 13 months and 1,472 minutes of League football.

His close range header after Schmeichel had palmed out a Jim Magilton chip stunned a packed Old Trafford into silence. But after already missing a series of chances, United were back on level terms and in the hunt for the championship after just 21 minutes.

An innocuous looking cross spread total panic in the visitors' defence and when Monkou and Charlton tied themselves in a tangle of legs, Cole pounced for his 12th strike in just 16 starts.

It was all the encouragement United needed to launch a wave of attacks and although Southampton did their bit for former team-

---

MANCHESTER UNITED 2

SOUTHAMPTON 1

(Half-time score : 1-1)

United: Schmeichel, Irwin, Bruce, Sharpe, Pallister, Ince, McClair, Hughes (Scholes 76), Cole, Butt, Neville.
Subs: Beckham, Walsh.
Southampton: Beasant, Benali (Heaney 57), Magilton, Hall, Monkou, Le Tissier (Widdrington 76), Shipperley, Maddison, Charlton, Dodd, Watson.
Scorers: (United): Cole 21, Irwin 80 pen; (Southampton): Charlton 5.
Referee: P S Danson (Leicester).
Attendance: 43,479.

---

mates Alan Shearer, Tim Flowers and Jeff Kenna at Blackburn, it was United who always held the upper hand. Lee Sharpe, Mark Hughes and Steve Bruce could have all easily put the game beyond reach by half-time but their wastefulness ensured a tense night.

Gordon Watson and Neil Shipperley had both fired warning shots across United bows with good efforts and the clock seemed to be ticking away.

But then came the moment that changed the course of this game and possibly the title destiny. Quicksilver Cole ran on to Irwin's through-ball to sneak behind the Southampton defence and Monkou was forced to resort to an illegal shirt tug to restrain the striker as he charged in on goal.

Irwin stepped up to fire the penalty home and the delight of the United players as they conducted their lap of honour around Old Trafford was understandable after they had skirted so close to disaster.

League Table After Match

	P	W	D	L	F	A	Pts
Blackburn	41	27	8	6	79	37	89
Man Utd	41	26	9	6	76	27	87
Nottm Forrest	41	22	10	9	70	41	76
Liverpool	40	20	11	9	63	33	71
Newcastle	41	19	12	10	64	45	69
Leeds	40	19	12	9	55	36	69
Tottenham	40	16	13	11	64	54	61
QPR	41	16	9	16	58	57	57
Wimbledon	41	15	10	16	46	63	55
Southampton	41	12	17	12	59	61	53
Arsenal	41	13	12	16	51	47	51
Chelsea	41	12	15	14	48	54	51
Man City	41	12	13	16	51	61	49
Sheff Wed	40	12	12	16	45	55	48
Aston Villa	41	11	14	16	50	55	47
West Ham	40	12	10	18	40	47	46
Everton	40	10	16	14	43	51	46
Coventry	40	11	13	16	41	61	46
C Palace	40	11	12	17	31	43	45
Norwich	41	10	12	19	36	53	42
Leicester	41	6	10	25	43	78	28
Ipswich	40	7	6	27	35	88	27

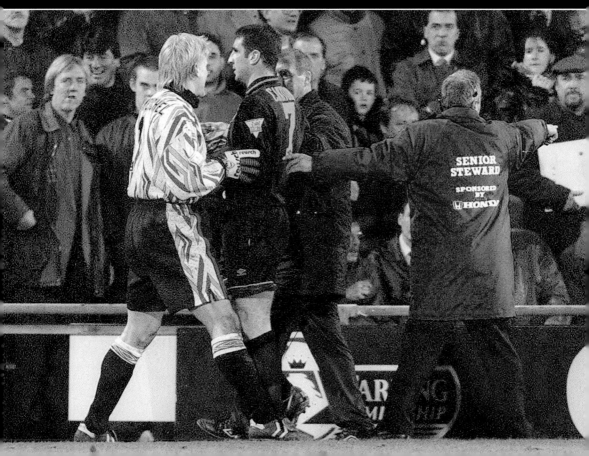

A bruised Andy Cole takes the applause after his first goal against Aston Villa.

Two of a Kind

Right and below Celebrations against Leeds in the FA Cup in February.

Opposite page (top) The eighth goal – from Ince – in the record-breaking 9-0 victory over Ipswich.

Opposite page (bottom) Hughes's second.

Clash of the

Titans

Right A clash between Bruce and Arsenal's Ian
Wright which was later to be restaged in the
players' tunnel.

Below Hughes scores against Arsenal.

Opposite page (top) Wimbledon's keeper Hans
Segers is helpless as Steve Bruce steams past to
score against the Dons.

Opposite page (bottom) Jamie Redknapp grabs
a goal against United.

The Late Run …

Above Coventry's Jonathan Gould fails to stop Andy Cole from scoring a vital goal against City.

Right Alex Ferguson in joyous mood as he celebrates the win over Coventry with assistant Brian Kidd.

Opposite page (top and bottom) A spectacular save from Schmeichel and a goal from Ince result in a win against Leicester.

May 14

Andy Cole will be haunted forever by two simple chances he fluffed in the final few minutes as the Championship slipped agonisingly away.

In one of the most dramatic conclusions to a league season, United did everything but score the goal which would have made them the fourth side in history to win three championships in succession.

Even into injury time Mark Hughes might have won the glory for United, but his shot – amid the most frantic of goalmouth scrambles – was blocked by the wall of West Ham defenders.

United manager Alex Ferguson denied afterwards that he had blundered in demoting Hughes to substitute. But maybe there will always be the nagging thought at the back of his mind that the decision was wrong. Certainly, Hughes' introduction after half-time galvanised United to their stirring performance.

United had begun the match knowing they needed the help which arrived from Liverpool but that was immaterial unless they coped with the diddymen of West Ham. The Hammers midfield must be the smallest in history, three at 5ft 7ins, with Ian Bishop the giant at 5ft 9ins. Two of the mini marvels combined to create the first goal on the half hour when Matt Holmes was given an ocean of space to collect a throw in from the left.

He turned smartly and delivered a routine cross which Michael Hughes despatched into goal on the volley from 10 yards with the minimum of fuss. The tiny winger didn't even have to ward off a challenge to tuck away his second goal.

United's first-half attacks lacked focus and apart from a drive against the post by Cole they never looked threatening.

Ferguson introduced Hughes after the break – and it brought immediate results. The Welshman was at the hub of incessant attacks by United, although the equaliser came from the simplest of free-kicks.

Gary Neville drifted in a cross from the right and Brian McClair, completely unmarked, powered a bullet header past the helpless Ludo Miklosko.

Just as news of Blackburn's first-half goal had seemed to deflate United, so the jubilation on the terraces which marked Liverpool's

---

WEST HAM 1

MANCHESTER UNITED 1

(Half-time score : 1-0)

West Ham: Miklosko, Breacker, Reiper, Potts, Rowland, Hughes (Webster 88), Bishop, Moncur, Hutchison (Allen 84), Morley, Holmes.
United: Schmeichel, Irwin, Sharpe, Pallister, Ince, McClair, Bruce, Keane (Scholes 77), Cole, Butt (Hughes 46), Neville.
Sub: Walsh.
Scorers: (West Ham): Hughes 31; (United): McClair 52.
Referee: A B Wilkie (Chester le Street).
Attendance: 24,783.

League Table After Match

	P	W	D	L	F	A	Pts
Blackburn	42	27	8	7	80	39	89
Man Utd	42	26	10	6	77	28	88
Nottm Forrest	42	22	11	9	72	43	77
Liverpool	42	21	11	10	65	37	74
Leeds	42	20	13	9	59	38	73
Newcastle	42	20	12	10	67	47	72
Tottenham	42	16	14	12	66	58	62
QPR	42	17	9	16	61	59	60
Wimbledon	42	15	11	16	48	65	56
Southampton	42	12	18	12	61	63	54
Chelsea	42	13	15	14	50	55	54
Arsenal	42	13	12	17	52	49	51
Sheff Wed	42	13	12	17	49	57	51
West Ham	42	13	11	18	44	48	50
Everton	42	11	17	14	44	51	50
Coventry	42	12	14	16	44	62	50
Man City	42	12	13	17	53	64	49
Aston Villa	42	11	15	16	51	56	48
C Palace	42	11	12	19	34	49	45
Norwich	42	10	13	19	37	54	43
Leicester	42	6	11	25	45	80	29
Ipswich	42	7	6	29	36	93	27

equaliser gave Ferguson's side Churchillian inspiration.

Miklosko made two fantastic saves to keep out headers from Lee Sharpe and Hughes, and every corner seemed to bring a goalmouth scramble.

Not that West Ham faded away. Peter Schmeichel bravely saved at the feet of Holmes as he steamed into the box, and Denis Irwin fly-hacked away inside the six yard box as Don Hutchison prepared to score.

The action never ceased through. Steve Bruce was booked for dissent when he claimed United should have had a penalty, and so was Hughes for an off the ball tussle with Hutchison. But this was not the snarling United so heavily criticised this season. This was a totally committed team, shrugging off the disgraceful booing of Paul Ince by the West Ham fans, to produce the most heart-warming, and ultimately most heart-breaking, spectacle.

Manchester's heads were bowed at the final whistle. Cole and co had blown it.

Bruce after the final whistle has blown.

May 20

Manchester United saw their season end without a trophy as the men who might have saved them sat helpless on the team bench. Eric Cantona, banned, Andrei Kanchelskis, injured, and Andy Cole, Cup-tied, were but frustrated spectators.

United played too much through the middle and not enough down the wider flanks where Lee Sharpe was peripheral and where Ryan Giggs reminded us only fleetingly of past glories. United's place in Europe which they desperately wanted to be the Champions' Cup is now merely the Uefa Cup, a sobering come-down after their two seasons of outstanding success.

Runners-up, whether it be the Premiership or the FA Cup, is not the benchmark manager Alex Ferguson has set and he admitted: "It is hard to take and the players are showing that in the dressing room. I am pleased to see that, because sometimes they forget what defeat is like. They know now."

For Everton there was only delight. We can recognise Neville Southall's courage, acknowledge Dave Watson's resilience, marvel at Ander Limpar's skills and salute Paul Rideout's goal. But what of Joe Royle? When the judgements are made on Everton's season, victory in the FA Cup final will be seen as the fulfilment of an impossible dream.

When Royle moved across from Oldham last November 11 what he found at Goodison was a battleground littered with broken men. He galvanised his demoralised troops for further action, instilling a conviction that hard work and raw aggression would bring restoration. He called his players his Dogs of War, a label that seemed appropriate at the time but which he now wishes to be struck from the CV. "We are no longer Dogs of War but winners at Crufts," he says.

At Wembley they fought on equal footing, scored a winning goal from a classic counter-attack when United were suicidally short of numbers at the back, and earned their conquest. The goal came in the 30th minute as Limpar collected the loose ball after Dave Watson robbed Ince and set Matt Jackson free. His pass inside gave Graham Stuart a clear shooting chance from the penalty spot, but with United spreadeagled he crashed his shot against the bar. The ball rebounded

---

EVERTON 1

MANCHESTER UNITED 0
(Half-time score : 1-0)

Everton: Southall, Jackson, Hinchcliffe, Watson, Ablett, Parkinson, Horne, Stuart, Rideout (Ferguson 51), Limpar (Amokachi 69), Unsworth.
United: Schmeichel, Irwin, Bruce (Giggs 46), Pallister, Neville, Sharpe (Scholes 73), Ince, Keane, Butt, McClair, Hughes.
Sub: Walsh.
Scorers: Rideout 30
Referee: G Ashby (Worcestershire)
Attendance: 79,592

perfectly for the advancing Rideout who beat off Irwin's desperate challenge to head into the empty net by the near post.

United never compensated for Giggs' failure to regain sufficient fitness to start the game. Without Kanchelskis they lacked width and pace, without Cole the finishing was blunt and without Cantona they had no fantasy. Giggs made a difference when he came on for hamstring-victim Steve Bruce but their second half comeback was not sharp enough to hold on to last season's prize.

Brian McClair had a looping header tipped onto the bar by Southall, who then saved twice as Scholes got in on the right. Scholes did not find it too amusing when Southall made the double save that could have extended the game, nor Gary Pallister when he clutched a goalbound header with sure hands.

Peter Schmeichel, who joined the United front-line in the last desperate moments, vowed that the Old Trafford men would be back with a vengeance. "I still think we're the best team in the country," said the Dane. "We've been hit by injuries and suspensions and so we've not had the consistency in terms of team selection which is the way to win what you deserve. "But if you look at the way our season has gone, to end up taking the championship to the last game and then to get to the FA Cup final a week later – that shows we're not a bad team."

Ferguson prefers to rely on wounded pride. "This is the first time for five years that we haven't picked anything up and that's hard to take," he said. "We will be back...."

Neville Southall saves Paul Scholes shot.

Great Matches

Of The Past

April 24, 1948

Matt Busby's 1948 Wembley side shone like a beacon. Captained by Irishman Johnny Carey, a defender with the bearing and high principles of Busby himself, it boasted a magnificent forward line. Flying Scot Jimmy Delaney played on the right wing with Charlie Mitten, one of the sweetest strikers of the ball in the game, on the left. The dashing Jack Rowley was a traditional centre-forward with a fierce shot. He was complemented perfectly by the subtle, high-scoring Stan Pearson at inside-left and clever young Johnny Morris at inside-right.

Mitten, wing-half Henry Cockburn and Morris were brilliant, capricious spirits while Rowley, Pearson and Delaney were more apt to toe the line. Meanwhile centre-half Allenby Chilton and goalkeeper Jack Crompton were utterly dependable.

United were still playing home games at Maine Road as bomb-ravaged Old Trafford was being rebuilt but it did not stop them entrancing post-war England. Busby's side were not to be champions that

MANCHESTER UNITED 4
BLACKPOOL 2

United: Crompton, Carey, Aston, Anderson, Chilton, Cockburn, Delaney, Morris, Rowley, Pearson, Mitten.
Scorers: (United): Rowley (2), Pearson, Anderson. (Blackpool): Shinwell (penalty), Mortensen.
Attendance: 100,000

Johnny Carey.

Jack Rowley.

season. Arsenal were grinding their way towards the League title. But it was United who were celebrated across the land with their spontaneity and exuberance.

En route to Wembley United had beaten Aston Villa 6-4 away, Liverpool 3-0 at neutral Goodison, Charlton 2-0 at neutral Huddersfield, Preston 4-1 at Maine Road and Derby 3-1 in the Hillsborough semi-final. Now loomed Blackpool and opponents of the calibre of Stan Mortensen, Harry Johnston and a 33-year-old legend named Stanley Matthews.

Blackpool tore up the script after 12 minutes. Mortensen broke through for a clear view of goal when brought down by Chilton in the penalty area. Eddie Shinwell beat Crompton with the spot kick. United responded furiously but were a shade lucky with the equaliser in the 28th minute. A misunderstanding between Blackpool goalkeeper Joe Robinson and centre-half Eric Hayward let Rowley in to walk the ball over the line.

The irrepressible Mortensen hammered Blackpool in front again in the 35th minute. Busby's composure at the interval was remarkable. He insisted that if United kept playing their natural passing game their superior technique would win the day. In the 69th minute, after punishing United pressure, Blackpool finally cracked as Rowley headed in a free-kick from the quick-thinking Morris.

Crompton saved brilliantly from Mortensen and within seconds the ball was in the Blackpool net. The United keeper's clearance was switched by Johnny Anderson to Pearson who scored off the post from 25 yards minutes from the end. Three minutes later Anderson's shot from 35 yards was deflected and it was 4-2. No one could remember a team coming from behind twice to win the Cup.

Next day 100,000 Mancunians thronged United's coach as it crawled through the city to the town hall in Albert Square. Of that Wembley line-up seven were locals. They were as Manchester in character as King Cotton himself. Their bonus for winning what is still acclaimed as the most famous Cup final of all was £20.

February 6, 1957

This was the game in which Matt Busby's newly styled Babes gave the first real glimpse of the lodestone of Europe, the occasion when United supporters discovered a rich vein of Continental nights that continue to dazzle to the present day. Consider the scene as those fans of the Fifties in their grey macs and duffel coats, their mufflers and trilbies, filed in their legions to the floodlit Maine Road.

Old Trafford would not be equipped with lights until the next round, so it was the home of neighbours Manchester City that illuminated United's first steps in Europe. Twelve months before their appalling destruction at Munich the Babes were climbing towards their zenith. The names trip off the tongue even today. Colman, Byrne, Taylor and Viollet and the most competitive young wing-half in Europe in Duncan Edwards. Hammering on the door was a kid named Bobby Charlton.

In their first European season the Babes had slaughtered the Belgian champions Anderlecht 12-0 in the preliminary round tie with 10 of the goals coming at Maine Road. The Belgian captain Mermans insisted afterwards: "They should pick this whole team for England." That opinion was reinforced as United beat the German champions Borussia Dortmund 3-2 on aggregate in the next round.

But Bilbao looked a different sort of Continental beast. The trip to northern Spain in January was a nightmare. Snow had closed the airport when United arrived. The Spaniards, beaten at home only once in three seasons, won the first leg 5-3 on a pitch sodden by 48 hours of rain and sleet. A valiant final flourish from Billy Whelan, who struck a goal of wicked power late on, gave United a chance in the return leg. But could they take it?

Henry Rose, that most emotive of all football reporters of the Fifties and a quintessential Mancunian, captured the passion of their response in the first two paragraphs of his *Daily Express* report.

"My hands still tremble as I write. My heart still pounds. And a few hours have passed since with 65,000 other lucky people I saw the greatest soccer victory in history. Hammering in my brain, almost shattering my senses, is the still fresh memory of the spectacle of 11 brave, gallant footballers battering, pounding until they had on their knees almost crying for mercy a team of Spaniards ranked as one of

---

MANCHESTER UNITED 3

ATLETICO BILBAO 0

(United won 6 - 5 on aggregate)

United: Wood, Foulkes, Byrne, Colman, Jones, Edwards, Berry, Whelan, Taylor, Viollet, Pegg.
Scorers: Viollet, Taylor, Berry.
Attendance: 65,000

Duncan Edwards

the best club sides in the world."

What Henry Rose saw that night was the ultimate evidence that Busby had within his dressing-room the best group of young players in the history of the game in England. The Basques were tough. They had come to battle, selecting an extra defender, Etura, to replace Uribe, who had scored twice in the first leg. For 42 minutes Bilbao put up the shutters. Then Edwards, driving forward more fiercely than anyone, created the chance for Dennis Viollet to score .

Could United get another two goals? The portents did not at first look good. Viollet twice had the ball in the net within three minutes of the restart and both strikes were disallowed. Bilbao, galvanised by their international centre-half Jesus Garay, did not buckle even when Tommy Taylor hit the post. But 20 minutes from time the irrepressible Taylor, accepting a quick free-kick from Colman, scored. Now it was an aggregate draw. With six minutes left and Maine Road in uproar Taylor surged past Garay on the right and pushed a short ball back to Berry, who stroked in the aggregate winner. United were through to the semi finals of the Champions' Cup. The Bilbao captain Piru Gainza admitted: "They play with such passion we were simply overwhelmed."

The Spaniards had been on a bonus of several hundred pounds a man to win. Busby's flamboyant youngsters, the greatest attraction of their generation, received appearance money of £5 each and £3 win bonus. The maximum wage had increased to £15 so they received £23 in their pay packets the following Friday. It had been a good week.

Matt Busby's Babes.

February 19, 1958

Two weeks after the air crash that destroyed the United team 59,848 supporters filed into Old Trafford bonded by a grief that flooded out from this corner of industrial England across the nation. They were there to mourn of course. But their presence at the delayed FA Cup fifth-round tie against Sheffield Wednesday also echoed the national will that United must rise again.

But would anything ever be the same? With Matt Busby lying critically injured in Munich's Rechts der Isar hospital Jimmy Murphy stepped into the biggest crisis any football manager has ever countenanced. The coffins had returned from Munich to rest in the gym at Old Trafford as Busby's irascible assistant set about the job of waking those left from the nightmare around them.

He had a formidable personality, this Welshman who had worked in Busby's shadow, and he was to need it in the days ahead. Murphy was helped in his task by Jack Crompton who left his coaching job at Luton to lift the shattered morale of survivors who could still not come to terms with the devastation.

The FA, like the rest of the nation, recognised the scale of the tragedy and allowed United to postpone the Sheffield Wednesday tie. The crash 14 days earlier had killed Roger Byrne, David Pegg, Tommy Taylor, Eddie Colman, Mark Jones, Billy Whelan and Geoff Bent as well as coach Bert Whalley, trainer Tom Curry and secretary Walter Crickmer. The country's finest player, Duncan Edwards was to succumb to appalling injuries two days later.

When the gates closed on those 59,848 inside Old Trafford several thousand more stood outside. Murphy had already started to put together the pieces. He paid Blackpool £8,000 for their 33-year-old midfield driver Ernie Taylor. Murphy also signed Stan Crowther, Aston Villa's hard-tackling wing-half. The deal cost United £23,000 and, though he was Cup-tied, having played for Villa in the third round, the FA agreed to waive their rule.

As the big crowd waited for the teams to appear the atmosphere was stunned by grief. But at this most sombre moment in the history of Old Trafford were sown the seeds of revival. In a moving match programme message under the heading 'United Will Go On' chairman

MANCHESTER UNITED 3
SHEFFIELD WEDNESDAY 0

United: Gregg, Foulkes, Greaves, Goodwin, Cope, Crowther, Webster, Taylor, Dawson, Pearson, Brennan.
Scorers: Brennan (2), Dawson.
Attendance: 59,848

Harold Hardman wrote: "Although we mourn our dead and grieve for our wounded we believe that our great days are not done for us.

The sympathy and encouragement of the football world, and particularly our supporters, will justify and inspire us. The road back may be long and hard but, with the memory of those who died at Munich, of their stirring achievements and wonderful sportsmanship ever with us . . . MANCHESTER UNITED WILL RISE AGAIN."

Even after such a message, with its ringing tones of heroic defiance, it could still have been a dreadful experience for everyone at Old Trafford that night. Murphy had been unable to give the programme editor a team. Instead there were 11 blank spaces to fill. Bill Foulkes and Harry Gregg led the team out and there was a huge response from the crowd at the sight of the two Munich survivors.

The side contained two debutants from the A team: Irish boy Shay Brennan, a wing-half converted to outside-left for the night, and Mark Pearson who had been plucked from the youth team. Five reserves completed the line-up with Crowther and Taylor. Sheffield Wednesday were no mean opponents with the England internationals 0Redfern Froggatt and young captain Albert Quixall.

The portents for a scratch United were not good. But the sheer emotion of the occasion overwhelmed Wednesday and Murphy's hastily assembled team won 3-0. Brennan scored direct from a corner in the 27th minute and added another goal with half-an-hour left. Then Alex Dawson ensured United's place in the sixth round a few minutes before the end of an extraordinary night. Murphy's revival work had begun.

March 9, 1966

Stepping off the flight from Lisbon George Best was photographed wearing a sombrero. Next day the picture of "El Beatle" was projected across the nation and Continent. Young, handsome and sexy Georgie Best became overnight the epitome of England's Swinging Sixties. Life would never be the same for him again.

Carnaby Street, the Beatles, the Rolling Stones and now professional football's first pop star. The previous night Best had silenced a 75,000 crowd in the Stadium of Light, ripping apart one of Europe's great sides. Benfica had Eusebio, whose lithe, spectacular style epitomised the joy of the game. Before the 10 p.m. kick off with rockets lighting up Lisbon's night sky, Eusebio had been presented with a statuette to mark his selection as European Footballer of the Year. He had formidable team mates like Coluna, Torres and Agusto. There was no hint of the devastation to come.

The Portuguese had a narrow 3-2 defeat at Old Trafford in the first leg. The one goal advantage was little enough for United to take to Lisbon. Yet it was all over almost before the big crowd could draw breath. Best, just 19, scored in the 6th and 12th minutes. John Connelly got the third two minutes later from a Best pass. The fans couldn't believe what they were seeing.

Never before had a foreign side scored more than two goals in the Estadio de Lus.

But it was the manner of Benfica's destruction that jolted mid-sixties Europe. United, the club who almost died at Munich eight years earlier, were back as one of the Continent's great sides. Best headed the opener from a pinpoint free kick by Tony Dunne. Goalkeeper Costa Pereira was stranded in no-man's land as the ball soared into the top corner. Then came the goal for which Best was to be remembered on the Continent for a generation.

Harry Gregg's mighty clearance sped two thirds the length of the field. David Herd nodded the ball back. And Best streaked away spurting past two white shirted defenders as if they were statues before luring the 'keeper and hitting a swift right foot shot low into the corner. It was the stuff of fantasy. Denis Law quickly masterminded number three, working the ball in from the deep, drawing

BENFICA 1

MANCHESTER UNITED 5

(United win 8 - 3 on aggregate)

United: Gregg, Brennan, Dunne, Crerand, Foulkes, Stiles, Best, Law, Charlton, Herd, Connelly.
Scorers: Best (2), Connelly, Crerand, Charlton.
Attendance: 75,000.

defenders, slipping a pass to Best who played it on for Connelly to ram it home.

In the second half right back Shay Brennan sliced into his own goal. But with the aggregate score at 6-3 there was no alarm in Busby's side. With 12 minutes left Pat Crerand shot United's fourth starting an exodus of thousands of Portuguese fans from their famous stadium. They couldn't stomach the first ever European home defeat of their beloved Eagles. Finally Bobby Charlton waltzed through for a dazzling fifth.

Law, the Demon King of Old Trafford's soaring sixties, said: "Two years earlier we had been beaten 5-0 by Lisbon in the Cup Winners Cup. When we went out all the Portuguese fans were holding out their hands with all five fingers extended giving us the salute. To say we were keyed up was an understatement.

"I wasn't exactly pleased in the dressing-room beforehand when Pat Crerand, kicking a ball about, banged it against a mirror. The glass shattered and though no-one said anything I imagine everyone was thinking about seven years bad luck. Yet we went out and were three goals up in the first quarter of an hour. It was the best performance in my view from a United team in Europe. It was a beautiful experience and a joy to share in that splendid team effort."

The most apt postscript came from Best. There were great days ahead for United's young superstar. Two years later he was to help United win the European Cup by beating these same opponents. But even as United flew home from Lisbon the portents of a career that veered between greatness and tragedy were there. "That night changed it all. Life from then on started to become crazy" he said.

May 6, 1967

If anyone needed proof that Busby had created something special from the Swinging Sixties it came in this famous late-season dismantling exercise in East London. Galvanised by the holy trinity of Best, Law and Charlton, United clinched the title with a game to spare, confirming their right to stand alongside Busby's great sides of 1948 and 1957.

United had crushed everything in their path at Old Trafford before gates averaging 53,800. But this was the biggest destruction on opposition soil of any side that season. Their relentless mood was encapsulated by an incident near the end.

With the sixth goal lodged in West Ham's net Nobby Stiles trotted over to Bill Foulkes and said: "Congratulations, Bill, on your fourth championship medal." All Nobby got in response was a rollicking and an order to concentrate on the game.

The opposition so comprehensively mangled that day were no mere cannon fodder. West Ham boasted in Moore, Hurst and Peters three World Cup players. They had won the European Cup Winners' Cup two years earlier.

But the Londoners were in disarray from the moment Stiles thrust for goal in the second minute. The ball spun loose for Bobby Charlton to streak through a gap between two players and start the rout. Then, irresistibly, Pat Crerand, Bill Foulkes and George Best sliced through to put United four up in the first 25 minutes.

In the second half Denis Law, the great Demon King of Old Trafford, caught fire. He scored twice, once from the penalty spot. At the end the West Ham fans knew they had witnessed something special. The balance of that 1966-67 United side was perfect, their technique honed by great players at the peak of their powers.

The title had not been a cake-walk. Busby had to overcome the loss of David Herd, who broke his leg against Leicester City on March 18 in the act of scoring his 16th league goal. It could have been a calamity. Herd was one of the unsung heroes of Old Trafford, having reeled off league goal tallies of 14, 19, 20, 20 and 24 before that bad fracture.

It was with some anxiety that Busby waited to see whether his side could get by without Herd's strike power. He need not have worried.

WEST HAM 1
MANCHESTER UNITED 6
(Half-time score : 4-0)

United: Stepney, Brennan, Dunne, Crerand, Foulkes, Stiles, Best, Law, Sadler, Charlton, Aston.
Scorers: (United): Charlton, Crerand, Foulkes, Best, Law (2)
Attendance: 53,800

Law, with 23 goals from 36 league games, remained the fulcrum of United's sparkling attack. Best was unstoppable on the right flank; Charlton moved up a gear late in the season. And in midfield Pat Crerand delivered passes to the world-class performers in front with slide-rule accuracy.

Busby still had to make an important tactical switch, though, to cover Herd's absence, pushing Stiles into attack and pulling David Sadler back from the forward line to form a fine double centre-half pairing with Foulkes. It was a key ploy. Though United's attack dazzled everyone, their defence was the rock on which Best, Law, Charlton and the young left-winger John Aston performed their histrionics.

Backed by goalkeeper Alex Stepney, a remarkable £50,000 September bargain from Chelsea, the side had a brilliant left-back in Irishman Tony Dunne and effective stop-gaps like Noel Cantwell, Shay Brennan and the young Bobby Noble. Regrettably Noble, one of United's great home-grown talents, missed the last three games. A car crash close to his Stockport home ended his career.

The players all had their own ideas about why they had won the championship. Crerand thought the absence of European games and being knocked out of the Cup early were crucial. "There were no Wednesday matches to worry about, no race against time to get players fit," he said. "By Saturday everybody was bursting to play. There was no pressure. It was our easiest season."

This was typically droll stuff from the Glaswegian. Best insisted United's harder mental attitude away from Old Trafford was the difference. What is certain is that in his 21st year as manager Busby had pulled together a side who showed on a May day in East London the deadly destructive arts of football masters.

May 29, 1968

Downstairs Joe Loss and his orchestra played on. But in his room at London's Russell Hotel Bobby Charlton was out like a light. Five times he tried to get to his feet. Five times he failed.

Three hours earlier he had helped Manchester United win the European Cup at Wembley.

"I missed most of the celebrating that night. I was absolutely drained and kept fainting," said Charlton. "I couldn't make the reception. My wife Norma told me that Matt had got up late in the evening to sing 'What a wonderful world'. I guess that just about summed it up for all of us."

Though Busby and Charlton had salted Wembley's turf with their joyful tears the brutal truth was that by that May night in 1968 United were past their Sixties' peak. Manchester City had won the league. It was the last chance Matt Busby would have of crowning his career.

Charlton had been in on Busby's great European adventure almost from the start. He was convinced their joint destiny was to be fulfilled. The humidity was uncomfortable. But Charlton sensed United would find something extra. The commodity was resilience.

Had they not pulled back from 3-1 down to draw 3-3 with Real Madrid in the Bernabeu Stadium in the semi-final and gone through 4-3 on aggregate?

Before the night was over their resilience was to end years of trial and tragedy and put the European Cup in Busby's grasp. The match went ahead without Denis Law. He had undergone a knee operation, so one of the three great players of Busby's side had to watch the game on TV in hospital.

It started slowly for tension was acute and the reward great. Benfica detailed Cruz to stop Best and half a dozen times in the first half the wispy United forward was hurled to the turf.

It needed a goal from Charlton to set the game alight in the 53rd minute. From Sadler's cross his glancing header flew into the far corner of the net. The deadlock was broken.

The game's outstanding players were not Best or Charlton but John Aston, on the left-wing, and Nobby Stiles, confirming again his reputation as one of the great markers of his era. Charlton compared him to "a sheepdog keeping everything under control. If one of the sheep

MANCHESTER UNITED 4

BENFICA 1

*(After extra time :
Half-time score : 1-1)*

United: Stepney, Brennan, Dunne, Crerand, Foulkes, Stiles, Best, Kidd, Charlton, Sadler, Aston.
Scorers: (United): Charlton 2, Best, Kidd; (Benfica): Graca.
Attendance: 100,000

George Best.

tried to break away he would dart into action and put him back in the pen".

Nine minutes from the end of normal time Torres, Benfica's giant centre-forward, climbed above United's defence to glance the ball to Graca, who levelled the score.

United's defence, which had dealt with the twin threats of Eusebio and Torres brilliantly, began to creak. Twice Eusebio broke through in the closing minutes and twice Alex Stepney saved his shots. Had he remained composed Eusebio would have finished United. But he went for glory and tried to break the net.

So it was extra time. Busby told his men: "If you pass the ball to each other you'll beat them." No more dramatic opening to the last half-hour could have been imagined. United swept forward and twice in two minutes they scored. Stepney's clearance was headed on by Brian Kidd to Best, who carved one of his great goals, taking the ball round two defenders and the keeper before popping it into the net. Then it was Kidd, heading into the net after his first attempt was beaten out by keeper Henrique. Benfica were broken. But United were not finished. Charlton brilliantly curled United's fourth beyond Henrique's reach from Kidd's pass.

David Sadler recalls looking at Matt Busby at that night's banquet: "The boss looked very old, which he had never seemed before. There was a sense that this was the end of something momentous . . . I wondered if there was anywhere to go from here . . ."

Celebration time.

March 21, 1984

Bryan Robson led United out for this famous hard day's night in Europe with something to prove. He finished the game carried shoulder high from the pitch after one of the epic performances of the Eighties.

The best player of Ron Atkinson's Old Trafford management had missed two easy chances in the 2-0 defeat in the first leg in the Nou Camp. Robson didn't shirk responsibility. He said he was to blame for the defeat. "Big games are about putting the ball in the back of the net and a player of my experience should have done that," he said. Honest and fearless, he dug deeper into his reserves of character, stamina and courage than anyone at Old Trafford.

As a teenager Robson had genuinely worried about his lack of physique. Would he be strong enough, big enough for professional football? Those doubts were conquered by more than the traditional steak diet. His career was built on an inner strength that kept him going though bones were broken and tissue torn with monotonous regularity.

Even so no one in the 58,547 crowd anticipated that the United and England captain was about to turn this night into a personal mission. Barcelona had Diego Maradona, the best player in the world, in their attack. But here the Argentinian, suffering from a thigh injury, was a mere bit-part player.

The night belonged to the likes of Remi Moses, who worked around Maradona like a terrier in a rabbit warren. It was about Ray Wilkins' midfield brain and the splendid running of Frank Stapleton and Norman Whiteside in attack that breached the Spaniards' rugged offside trap.

Above all it belonged to Robson. The early goal United desperately needed came in the 22nd minute. Wilkins curled the ball in, Whiteside nodded on and Robson pounced to head past Urruti.

United then launched into a series of sweeping attacks that broke the Spaniards beyond recovery in the 50th and 52nd minutes. Again Robson was the penalty-box predator, scoring from close range after Urruti failed to hold a shot from Wilkins. With the big crowd in full cry Whiteside headed a cross back to the near post from where

MANCHESTER UNITED 3
BARCELONA 0
*(Half-time score : 1-0
United won 3 - 2 on aggregate)*

United: Bailey, Duxbury, Albiston, Wilkins, Moran, Hogg, Robson, Muhren, Stapleton, Whiteside, Moses.
Scorers: Robson (2), Stapleton.
Attendance: 58,547

Stapleton powerfully drove in United's third. There was bedlam but the game was not over yet. Barcelona's German midfielder Schuster pushed his side forward in a finale that saw United's young sub Mark Hughes fell Gerardo in the box. Every heart in the huge crowd stopped. But the Italian referee waved aside the penalty appeal and United were through to their first European semi-final for 15 years.

Atkinson described the 3-2 aggregate win as the best result of his career and the shock waves of Robson's performance lapped across Europe. The Italians were particularly taken with the United captain. Even when United tagged him with what they considered to be a prohibitive £3 million fee speculation about a move abroad continued through the summer.

So it was a huge relief to the supporters when in October of the following season club and player agreed a new seven-year contract. Robson was 27 and that decision effectively tied him to Old Trafford for the rest of his career.

The club chairman Martin Edwards said: "The length and worth of the contract is a record in Britain. At the same time there is an element of personal financial sacrifice by the player who could have kept himself available for a move to Italy at a later stage. We never really wanted to sell him in the summer and thought the £3 million price tag would frighten people off."

"We hope this contract makes it clear we want to keep our captain and most influential player. Bryan has made it just as clear that money is not everything to him either. It's a good contract but modest compared with Italian money. I cannot commend his attitude enough."

May 18, 1985

There was no way, surely, the occasion could fail to be a classic. Everton had won the league with five matches to spare. Howard Kendall's side had just lifted the European Cup Winners Cup. They were the best side in England and aiming for an historic treble.

As for United, Ron Atkinson's ball-playing team were undoubtedly the pick of the rest. Yet for most of the 120 minutes of this final the chemistry did not work. Atkinson versus Kendall would have been an unmitigated bore but for two remarkable episodes.

What transformed this match into one of the most gripping dramas of modern times was the tragedy of Kevin Moran's dismissal and the triumph of Norman Whiteside's extra-time winner for United.

It was Everton's 63rd game of a season that showed Kendall had put steel chords as well as abundant craft into his operation. They had the PFA Player of the Year in midfield general Peter Reid. They boasted the football writers' selection in keeper Neville Southall. They had bite up front from the fiery Andy Gray and great balance throughout.

United had great quality, too: Gordon Strachan and Jesper Olsen on the wings, Frank Stapleton and Mark Hughes striking and Whiteside and Bryan Robson digging from midfield. Such class should have produced a gem. Instead Wembley was bemused until the 77th minute by an undistinguished stalemate.

It was then that United centre-half Paul McGrath lost the ball to Reid just inside his own half to prompt the game's pivotal incident. As Reid rumbled towards goal Kevin Moran threw himself feet first at him. His right foot pushed the ball away. His left caught his opponent, sending him cartwheeling spectacularly.

Referee Peter Willis, a County Durham policeman, looked ominously officious. He lectured Moran and, as the United defender walked away, called him back. Astonishingly the tall man in black was pointing to the dressing-room. Within moments outrage swamped the United camp. Robson lambasted Willis. Moran beseeched him to change his mind, but there was no reprieve. The quiet Irishman was the first player to be sent off in a Cup Final at Wembley.

Instant TV replays showed the viewing millions Moran had pushed the ball away from Reid before making contact. It was the cruellest

---

MANCHESTER UNITED 1
EVERTON 0
(Half-time score : 0-0)

United: Bailey, Gidman, Albiston (Duxbury), Whiteside, McGrath, Moran, Robson, Strachan, Hughes, Stapleton, Olsen.
Scorer: Whiteside (110 mins)
Attendance: 100,000

decision in the history of English football, although Willis, admittedly, did not have the benefit of hindsight. His decision left United with 10 men 13 minutes from the end of normal time.

Suddenly anger welled up inside every red shirt and the sending-off started to work in their favour. For the first time that afternoon United's work was sharp and incisive. They dug in for extra time. The last half-hour was classic Cup-Final theatre. Everton went close. They poured forward and saw United captain Robson head against his own bar.

With 10 minutes left came the moment that confirmed Whiteside as arguably the best young player of Atkinson's Old Trafford era. Mark Hughes, in his own half, split the blue ranks ahead of him with a superb pass into space on the right. Whiteside pounded forward and, as Everton full-back Van den Hauwe stood off, moved purposefully into the corner of the box.

Whiteside turned inwards, the full-back stumbled and, with Southall's view momentarily obscured, the young Ulsterman curled a delicious cross-shot inside the far post with his left foot. Everton still made strenuous efforts to save the game in the few minutes left, but their dream of the treble was over.

When Moran went to collect his winner's medal he was told by an FA official it was being withheld. Next day the Irishman delighted the multitude of fans gathered in front of Manchester Town Hall with his oratory. Grabbing the microphone he declared: "We won the Cup for the supporters of Manchester United. You are the greatest in the world."

The story of his dismissal did not end there. The public outcry was fuelled by TV pictures confirming again there had been no malicious intent in his challenge. Several weeks later the FA dispatched his precious gong to Old Trafford.

April 4, 1988

This was a landmark game for Alex Ferguson's United capped by the most amazing managerial squabble ever witnessed at Anfield. Reporters gaped as two of the biggest personalities in football went for each other like Scottish fish wives.

Maybe it was the fact that Liverpool frittered a 3-1 lead against a United side reduced to 10 men for the last-half hour that inflamed the normally taciturn Kenny Dalglish. Perhaps it was Ferguson's realisation that his side had leaped a major psychological barrier that brought the blood rushing to his head.

"I can understand why clubs come away from here biting their tongues and choking on their own vomit knowing they have been done by the referees," rasped the United manager about Colin Gibson's dismissal for two bookings.

"You need a miracle here to win and I am not going on about this particular referee at all. But the whole intimidating atmosphere, the monopoly Liverpool have enjoyed for years, gets to you eventually."

Fergie was making his point to a radio reporter when Dalglish walked past carrying his six-week-old daughter Lauren in his arms.

"You might as well talk to my daughter. You will get more sense out of her," he blurted to the radio man. Ferguson reacted with an unprintable riposte.

All this came after a remarkable game. Liverpool had expected to win. They were the best side in England by a street with Hansen and Nicol in defence, sound midfield personnel like Houghton and McMahon and a world-class attack in Aldridge – Ian Rush was abroad with Juventus for the season – Barnes and Beardsley.

Ferguson's United had excellent individuals like Robson, McGrath, Whiteside, McClair, Strachan and Olsen but still lacked the style and panache of Dalglish's team. What they did not lack was persistence, and it kept them in Liverpool's slipstream to the end of the season, though Dalglish's side were still nine points clear when they landed the title.

That quality was never better demonstrated than in this sensational April day at Fortress Anfield. Bryan Robson revelled in such occasions. It was no coincidence that United's most combative player

---

LIVERPOOL 3

MANCHESTER UNITED 3

(Half-time score : 2-1)

United: Turner, Anderson, Blackmore (Olsen), Bruce, McGrath, Duxbury (Whiteside), Robson, Strachan, McClair, Davenport, Gibson.
Scorers: (United): Robson 3, 66, Strachan 77; (Liverpool): Beardsley 38, Gillespie 40, McMahon 47.
Attendance: 43,497.

shaped a ferocious, compelling contest by striking a goal in less than three minutes.

Liverpool fought back with superb aplomb and by the second minute of the second half were 3-1 ahead. Peter Beardsley equalised, Gary Gillespie headed number two from John Barnes' cross, and the 43,497 spectators were still shuffling back from the tea-bars when Steve McMahon went through a Mike Duxbury tackle and dispatched a 20-yard screamer for Liverpool's third.

No one gave Ferguson's side a prayer at that point. But the 54th-minute double substitution of Norman Whiteside and Jesper Olsen for Duxbury and Clayton Blackmore lit the blue touch-paper. United flared again.

Within four minutes Gibson was sent off by John Key for impeding Nicol. Earlier he had been booked for dissent but the dismissal for the double caution still looked harsh.

The incident brought an inspired response from United. The Kop was stunned as Robson pulled it back to 3-2 in the 66th minute with a deflected shot. Could they go one better and level it? Gordon Strachan came up with the answer in the 77th minute. Peter Davenport's classy chip over the home defence gave the tiny Scot the freedom of the Kop goalmouth and he streaked through to shoot past Bruce Grobbelaar.

No analysis of such an epic should ignore Whiteside's part. United's young Northern Ireland star relished nothing more than a collision with Liverpool at Anfield. He was lucky to escape punishment for elbowing Barnes and was eventually cautioned for a challenge on McMahon.

Anfield's reputation for impregnability first forged during the Shankly era had again been questioned by their biggest foes. The draw extended United's unbeaten record there to eight games stretching back to Boxing Day 1979.

The message from United captain Robson to the rest of the game was pointed: "At 3-1 Liverpool might have sat back a bit but it takes a lot to come back here when you are down to 10 men. It's up to other teams to play with a more positive attitude when they come here."

May 15, 1991

No one anticipated this European summit more eagerly than Mark Hughes. For three weeks the media had pitched it as Sparky's Revenge. The final in which United's Welsh warrior would at last prove Barcelona wrong.

"At first I tried to play it down because the past is the past. But deep down I welcomed this chance to show that in the right team I was better than they thought," admitted Hughes.

Undoubtedly the Nou Camp with its concrete cliffs and 100,000 crowds had daunted the younger Hughes. Recruited by Terry Venables from Old Trafford in 1986, he had a wretched time in Spain. Two seasons later he was back in Manchester after retrieving some of his self-respect on loan to Bayern Munich. Barcelona had another manager, Johan Cruyff, in charge since Hughes' brief stay and a few new players. No matter, Sparky was out to make his point.

First Alex Ferguson had a major decision to make. England midfielder Neil Webb had been scratching for form. Mike Phelan, the industrious artisan, was selected instead of the inconsistent artist. Webb never forgave Ferguson.

The United boss had other worries. Goalkeeper Les Sealey was protecting a knee that had been badly gashed in the League Cup final defeat by Sheffield Wednesday less than a month earlier. The odds against the English Cup winners were stacked high.

Yet they went out that rainy night and comprehensively outplayed one of the most vaunted clubs in Europe. Their fans helped. The Rotterdam stadium had been solidly colonised by the English, and as rain slanted in their faces they sang their hearts out.

"As we warmed up I looked across at the Barcelona players and some of them were shivering. Whether it was the cool rain or nerves I'm not sure but I began to think perhaps they didn't fancy the match as much as we did," said Hughes.

Barcelona's early passing was more precise but United went in at the interval looking a shade stronger. In the dressing-room Ferguson remained calm, urging his men to cash in with a goal while they were on top.

Twenty minutes into the second half they responded. Bryan Robson,

---

MANCHESTER UNITED 2

BARCELONA 1

(Half-time score : 0-0)

United: Sealey, Irwin, Bruce, Pallister, Blackmore, Phelan, Ince, Robson, Sharpe, McClair, Hughes.
Scorers: (United): Hughes 67, 75; (Barcelona): Koeman 83.
Attendance: 45,000

ruling midfield with force and fire, floated a free-kick forward after Hughes had been brought down. Steve Bruce met it with a firm header that was sailing towards goal when Hughes nipped in to give the ball a final push over the line.

Eight minutes later the Welshman came up with the emphatic stroke that clinched the match. Again it was Robson who created the chance with a ball chipped over the Barcelona defence. The Spanish keeper, Zubizaretta, came racing out. Hughes got there first, skipped past him but seemed to have knocked the ball too wide. The angle was acute. Most players would have rolled the ball carefully but not Hughes. He hammered it home with magnificent conviction.

"People ask me why I hit it so hard instead approaching the situation with more care," says Hughes. The short answer is 'I don't know' except to say I always try to make sure. I think, in fact, there were a couple of defenders racing back so my instinct was right . . ."

Ronald Koeman, Barcelona's Dutch midfield star, had been shackled brilliantly on this rainy Rotterdam night by Brian McClair and only managed to make a dent late on. Sealey's stitched knee had opened up again and he was clearly impeded as he moved late to Koeman's free-kick for Barcelona's goal. And Brian Laudrup might have equalised if Clayton Blackmore had not cleared off the line. But the whistle confirmed United's first European trophy since Wembley 1968.

The fans sensed Ferguson's side were gathering momentum, ready to challenge for the game's big pots again as Busby's had 23 years earlier. The motorcade next day from Manchester Airport should have taken two hours to get into the city centre. It took six hours as the fans' cameras flashed into the twilight. Hughes, more than anyone, was entitled to savour it all. "Some might say Barcelona were below par on the day but I am having none of that," he insisted much later. "People seem to forget that next season they won the European Cup."

The Players

Peter Schmeichel

Peter is acclaimed at Old Trafford as the best goalkeeper in Europe but 1995 was a year which changed Peter's philosophy on football and life.

The season was barely one month old when Peter felt an agonising pain in his back before the home match with Liverpool which United won 2-0. Peter took painkillers to get through the game but the next morning was in agony. "A disc was pressing on a nerve and for 10 days I was flat on my back. I couldn't sit or walk because of the pain," said Peter. The problem returned in the 3-0 home victory against Crystal Palace in November and this time Peter was forced to come off after a few minutes.

"My wife drove me home at half-time," said Peter. "The next few days when I was flat on my back I couldn't see myself ever playing again." In fact, the problem kept Peter sidelined for two months and that's why he regarded playing in the FA Cup final against Everton as a fantastic bonus.

"Ever since my injury my attitude to football and life has changed," he said. "Everything was routine and I moaned about training and extra matches. Now I am just so pleased to be fit again. When you think your career is over and suddenly you get bail, you appreciate everything so much more."

Peter, 31, whose nickname is The Terminator, was an Old Trafford fan as a youngster when he was enchanted by the glamour of Bobby Charlton and George Best. He signed for United in a £750,000 deal from Brondby in August 1991.

He has certainly come a long way from his Danish First Division days when he played almost like a sweeper behind the Brondby defence and was famous for taking as well as saving penalties. He was named 1990 Danish Player of the Year and won his first cap for Denmark against Greece in June 1987. He made his League debut for United against Notts County on the opening day of the 1991-92 season and was a commanding figure in Denmark's European Championship success in 1992.

Denis Irwin

Denis may be the quiet man of the Manchester United dressing room but there is no shortage of supporters when it comes to singing his praises.

Manager Alex Ferguson leads the appreciation society for the full-back who runs miles up and down the Old Trafford touchline in the overlapping role so crucial to United's success.

The Irish defender was offered a new three-year contract at the end of the 94-95 season which would take him up to the age of 33 and give him the chance of completing his career with the Reds."There's no problem with Denis playing for another three or four years", said Ferguson.

"He has always looked after himself and has been arguably our most consistent player for years."He has never been a minute's bother and has been a great buy. We watched him at Oldham all one season knowing that he would soon be out of contract. I was delighted to get him for £700,000."Irwin has been one of the rocks at the heart of the Republic of Ireland's defence and his former boss Joe Royle describes him as "the best full-back in the country."

Irwin, a strong tackler though at 5ft 7ins he is not a big man, was snapped up on a free transfer by Royle at Oldham when former Leeds boss Billy Bremner dumped him eight years ago. He became a big favourite at Boundary Park before Royle, under financial pressure, had to trade him four years ago.

Since then Irwin has developed into one of the champions' most consistent and dependable performers, missing just a handful of first team games.

Denis won his first cap for the Republic of Ireland against Morocco just two games after joining United. His strengths include his ability to get forward to support the attack and a blistering right-foot shot. He gets his fair share of goals and can be lethal with free kicks from the edge of the area. And no-one could forget his late blockbusting penalty which gave United a 2-1 victory over Southampton at Old Trafford to keep the Premiership pressure on Blackburn.

Gary Neville

With the unlucky Paul Parker injured for most of the season and David May also sidelined, 20-year-old Gary seized his chance to show he could perform with the very best in the Premiership.

He made more than 20 first team appearances, looking assured in defence and providing a new weapon in attack – a fearsome long throw-in.

The low point of his season came in the 3-2 away victory over Coventry when Gary was booked in the first minute for a foul on Coventry striker Peter Ndlovu. It meant Gary had reached 41 disciplinary points and though many of them had been collected in reserve team outings he was hauled before an FA disciplinary hearing.

For a while it seemed he might be ruled out of the FA Cup final but on May 11 the commission instead decided to fine him £1,000 and warn him about his future behaviour.

Gary, tall and athletic, comes from a sporting family. His younger brother Phil has already played in United's first team and Phil's twin Tracy is an England netball international.Gary's father, whose name really is Neville Neville, works for Bury Town as commercial manager and mother Jill makes it a family double there as secretary.

But Gary's heart is firmly at Old Trafford where he hopes to stay for years to come. "I've been watching United since I was five so it is a dream come true to play for them," he says. "I've still got a lot to learn but you can't fail with such quality players all around you."

Gary Pallister

Gary, as United's most consistent defender, does not score too many goals. But he does have a habit of scoring vital ones. None were more crucial than the one which earned United an FA Cup semi-final replay against Crystal Palace at Villa Park. A long throw from Gary Neville deep into extra-time and Pallister held off three Palace defenders to send a glancing header into the net at the far post. Pallister said:"I don't score many goals but that has to be the most important of my career. We were totally committed to getting a result. If you can't fight in a semi-final then you can't fight full-stop.

"We were not at our best so my goal was a real lifeline. Gary took

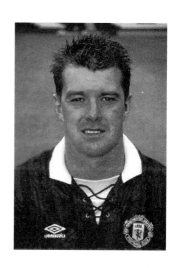

one of his massive throw-ins, which is such a dangerous weapon, and I got a flick. But it took an eternity to go into the net.

"I saw Eric Young throwing out one of his long legs and if anyone in football was going to get to it, it would have been big Eric. The lads all said it was agonising because it was like slow motion it took so long to go in.

"It was an eternity. My life flashed before me. But then it bounced up and over the line and the FA Cup was still up for grabs."

Gary conjured up another goal, again a header, in the replay to pay off another huge slice of the £2.3m fee which was a club record when he signed for United from Middlesbrough in August 1989. That looks more of a bargain as every season passes.

It's all a long way from the £60-a-week wages which Middlesbrough were reluctant to pay Gary when he joined them from non-league Billingham Town in 1984.

In his six years at United Gary – who won his first cap for England against Hungary in April 1988 – has proved his class as a dominant central defender, always comfortable playing the ball out of defence.

He was voted United's Player of the Year in his first season and voted Players' Player of the Year in 1991-1992. It's something of a dream come true for the boy who started work as a tea boy on an oil rig at 17 and whose sporting passion before soccer was cricket.

In fact, he was once a fast bowler for Junior League team Norton. He also has a reputation for being a bit of a prankster in the United dressing room.

Steve Bruce

Steve amassed more points than a few Premiership teams last season.

Unfortunately, they were all for falling foul of the referees' clampdown which was brought in after the World Cup.

The Old Trafford skipper was fined £750 and suspended for two games by an FA disciplinary commission after totalling 41 penalty points. It meant he missed United's first FA Cup semi-final against Crystal Palace and the Premiership clash with Leeds. But when he did play Steve was his usual, consistent self, scoring one of the most important goals of the season on a muddy night at Selhurst Park on March 7.

Just when it looked as if Wimbledon were going to hold United to a goalless draw Steve was thrown into the attack and cashed in on a blunder by goalkeeper Hans Segers.

Segers fumbled a cross from Brian McClair and Bruce was on hand to squeeze the ball through the keeper's legs, run around him and slot the ball into the empty net.

It was not the first time the evergreen Bruce had proved the match-winner for United, even though he is United's only non-international first-teamer. He spent most of his early career with Gillingham and then Norwich after Newcastle, Sunderland and Sheffield Wednesday all rejected him as a teenager. Ironically, they told him he was not tough enough.

"I played more than 200 League matches for Gillingham and when I got to the age of 23 I began to wonder whether I would ever kick a football in the top league. To have played for and to have captained the biggest club in the country has fulfilled my greatest dream."

Steve, a product of the famous Wallsend Boys' Club, moved to Norwich in August 1984 for £115,000 and to United in December 1987 for £800,000. He plays the odd game of golf and cricket for relaxation, is married to childhood sweetheart Janet and has two children.

Born on New Year's Eve he has a natural sense of goodwill and a nose to prove he is one of Britain's most courageous defenders at the last count it had been broken six times.

Paul Ince

Paul proved in 1995 what many soccer experts had been saying for years – he possesses all the midfield qualities to fill the gap at Old Trafford left by the departure of Bryan Robson.

It was such a pity that some powerful performances were overshadowed by the events surrounding Eric Cantona's kung fu kick at Selhurst Park.

Paul was one of the United players who went to help Cantona and was caught up in the crowd unrest which followed.

A fan subsequently made a complaint that he had been assaulted by Paul. Paul appeared before South Croydon magistrates on the same day as Cantona but opted for trial and was found innocent.

The case saw him lose his England place when manager Terry Venables left him out of the friendly with Uruguay. But if England could do without his talents some enterprising Italians were desperate to have Paul on their side.

Inter Milan's owner and president Massimo Maratti was prepared to spend £7m on Paul, saying: "Ince is a player of exceptional talent. He belongs in Italian football. I believe he will play at the top level in our game and the only surprise is that none of our rivals has so far realised that potential." Paul was a self-confessed East End tearaway as a teenager. His dad left the family home when he was a toddler, his mother went to Germany to become a waitress when he was 13 and Paul grew up with relatives.

Paul admits: "I was a sitting target for all the crooks in the neighbourhood. I hardly ever went to school. I used to stay in bed all day."

He was rescued by former West Ham boss John Lyall who brought him in to train with Hammers' youth team and acted as a father figure.

Paul spent two years in West Ham's reserves, made his League debut at 19 and, when Lyall was ousted as manager, left for Old Trafford in 1989. The initial move was called off when a groin problem was discovered at his medical.

A specialist's opinion eased concern, though United insisted on a reduced fee of £800,000 with payments of £8,000 per match for him over an agreed period. Paul, 27, was made England's first black captain in June 1993 against the United States in Boston an achievement he sees as a milestone for football as well as a personal triumph. Paul, who lives in the Cheshire stockbroker belt, is a great friend of boxer Frank Bruno and a cousin of Nigel Benn.

Roy Keane

Roy has the power, the pace and the all-round football acumen to play in just about any position.

He has had every opportunity to prove that in his two seasons at United when he has been needed to apply his defensive talents at full-back almost as often as his strong running and creative qualities in midfield. Unfortunately, his season will be best remembered for one act of recklessness in United's FA Cup semi-final replay against Crystal Palace at Villa Park. Roy needed seven stitches in an ankle injury after being the victim of a bad tackle in the first half. In hindsight he probably should not have come out for the second period for when he was aggressively tackled by Gareth Southgate he reacted by stamping on the prone Palace player.

The incident sparked ugly scenes with United and Palace players squaring up to each other. Roy was sent off along with Palace's Darren Patterson who had grabbed Roy by the throat after the initial incident.

Roy suffered an automatic three-match ban but was also charged by the FA with bringing the game into disrepute.

It was a punishment with which his Republic of Ireland boss Jack Charlton had some sympathy, especially as it kept Roy out of the European Championship qualifier with Portugal.

Charlton said: "I understand professional players. I know how they react. And he was reacting to a situation. There was nothing cynical or pre-meditated about it.

"Everyone was going on about what he had done and all his problems. He is a young lad. He gets on with his job. He's a good competitor. If you take away the competitiveness, ask him to stop and think, you have not got Roy Keane."Roy won the ball and when he turned round the guy came at him from a yard away and went through with two feet. It was nasty, totally out of order and he got away with it.

"To be actually cynical is one thing, but Roy just reacted. I still say to this day he didn't hurt the guy. He put his foot on him. He didn't stamp on him. He just put it there. He held back.

"I think people will react when they have nasty things done to them. If you cool him down for five or ten seconds he wouldn't do what he did."Roy's £3.75m transfer from Nottingham Forest to United was quite a meteoric rise for the boy who started playing for Irish side Cobh Ramblers just over six years ago for £40-a-week.

He comes from a footballing family: brothers Denis, Johnson and Pat all play local soccer in Ireland. None of them begrudge Roy his star-studded lifestyle and his mother Marie insists: "Roy was the one dedicated to soccer. He has lived for the game."

Outside soccer Keane loves listening to music plays a bit of snooker, and is toying with taking up Golf.

Mark Hughes

No player likes getting injured. But the knee damage Mark received when he collided with Newcastle goalkeeper Pavel Srnicek on January 15 probably saved his Manchester United career.

Mark had stormed in to score in typically courageous fashion when Srnicek's studs sliced open his knee and put on hold a proposed transfer to Everton. Mark had not been able to agree on the length of a new contract , though he was not happy at the prospect of leaving Old Trafford.

The injury, however, sidelined him for a month and in that time Eric Cantona was banned from football for his Kung Fu kick at Crystal Palace.

United could not afford to lose the striking talents of two special players. When Mark returned he promptly scored in the 3-1 FA Cup fifth round victory over Leeds United to stake a strengthening claim for an improved contract. United eventually agreed to a new two-year deal guaranteeing the Sparky magic would continue to grace the Theatre of Dreams. Mark, 30, comes from the Welsh village of Ruabon, near Wrexham, and is in his second spell at Old Trafford.

A product of United's youth policy Mark, who is 5ft 8ins and 12 stone, made his debut for United in 1983 and played 89 League games before catching the eye of Barcelona. He moved to join the then manager Terry Venables in what was at the time a British record £2.3 million.

However, he quickly found himself on loan to Bayern Munich. "The chance to go abroad probably came a bit too early for me," Mark admits. "I was only 23 at the time. It didn't really work out, but when

United bought me back two years later (for £1.8m) I was all the better for the experience. I enjoyed myself in Germany and will always be grateful to Uli Hoeness for getting me back on the rails. People say you should never go back but I am glad I did."

Mark, who gained six O-levels and once thought of going on to further studies, has twice won the PFA Player of the Year award. He lives in the Cheshire village of Prestbury with wife Jill and their two sons, Alex, 6, Curtis, 4, and two-year-old Xenna.

Lee Sharpe

United fans just love watching Lee race over to the corner flag, take the stick in his hand and pretend to sing the first few bars of Blue Suede Shoes.

His hip-shaking Elvis routine means he has scored another important goal and there were notable opportunities for him to practice his routine.

He took particular delight in scoring goals in Europe, – against IFK Gothenburg in September and Barcelona in October.

Lee first started his distinctive celebrations when he had a strike at ten-pin bowling. Now he considers himself the king of the goal dancers.

He wasn't doing much dancing during the middle part of the season, however, when he was sidelined with a hairline fracture of the ankle. Happily, it did not prove as damaging as the bout of meningitis or the hernia problem which had kept him out for large chunks of the previous two years.

Lee was a wiry 16-year-old YTS recruit with Torquay when he signed for United after Alex Ferguson had watched him in a midweek night match.

He cost just £60,000 down with further agreed payments and an exhibition match taking the completed transfer to £200,000. At first he was used as a left-back but his attacking career took off with a brilliant hattrick which helped beat Arsenal 6-2 in the Rumbelows Cup at Highbury in November 1990.

He won his first England cap as a substitute in a European Championship game against the Republic of Ireland in March 1991 and shortly afterwards was voted the PFA Young Player of the Year.

Lee comes from Halesowen, a suburb of Birmingham, though he now lives in a £400,000 executive home in Bowdon, Cheshire.

Andy Cole

Andy's £ 7m transfer from Newcastle to Old Trafford caught the football world completely by surprise. So much so that one Manchester local radio reporter, who received a tip-off the night before, dismissed it as being too far-fetched to broadcast. Everyone, however, was soon sitting up and taking notice of Andy's quickness of feet and all-round sharpness in front of goal.

Proof that United's money would reap a rich dividend came in Andy's seventh game at home to Ipswich when he crashed home five goals in a 9-0 victory which had Alex Ferguson proclaiming: "Andy is capable of anything."

That performance, the first goal of which took him past the 100 senior goals mark at the age of 23, was the best in United's 103-year League history.

It certainly gave Andy confidence, though he was quick to praise his teammates. "It was the most complete team performance I've ever been involved in," he said. "It was a ten out of ten and if the manager says that was the closest he has ever seen to perfection I'm happy to agree."

Andy's razor-sharp form did not go unnoticed at international level and when Blackburn's Alan Shearer pulled out of the England squad for the friendly against Uruguay in March Andy was called up for his first cap.

Unfortunately, he had to settle for a place on the bench but came on for Peter Beardsley in the 71st minute. Immediately he put some bite into a lacklustre England performance, hitting the bar with a flashing, instinctive header just a couple of minutes after coming on.

The goals continued to flow and Andy was in the thick of things as the Premiership race reached its finale. He scored the first goal against Southampton in the penultimate match and also won the penalty which took the title campaign to the final game.

And he did all that after hearing his girlfriend had given birth to a baby boy just 15 minutes before the kick-off.

Eric Cantona

United fans were delighted when Eric turned down an offer to join Inter Milan to stay with United for three more years in a deal worth £2m.

It was the culmination to another tempestuous chapter in the life of the flamboyant Frenchman which had seen his season come to a shuddering halt on Wednesday January 25 – the night he launched a kung-fu kick on a Crystal Palace supporter.

Cantona had just been sent off for the fifth time as a United player for aiming a kick at a Palace defender. As he was walking down the touchline with United kit manager Norman Davies, the fan rushed down 11 rows of seats and appeared to taunt the Frenchman.

Cantona launched himself at the fan with both feet and the fracas only subsided when stewards intervened.

Eric was charged with common assault and when the case came before South Croydon magistrates court he was sent to prison for two weeks – a sentence changed on appeal to 120 hours community service. The FA also banned him from all football until September 30, 1995. While he was getting away from it all with his family in Guadeloupe Eric also had a bust-up with ITN reporter Terry Lloyd, who was asking him for an interview on the beach.

It seems wherever Cantona goes, so do thrills and controversy in roughly equal measure. At least some people, however, benefited from the sorry affair – 700 Manchester children receiving coaching lessons over two months from one of the game's most extravagant talents.

The first session took place on April 18 when Eric put 12 boys aged between nine and 13 from Ellesmere Park Junior FC through their paces. Schoolboy midfield player Simon Croft turned to him for advice on coping with disciplinary pressures. Eric, clearly having learned from his experience, said a cool head was essential as he told the youngster: "If you're going to get a yellow card, walk away and don't get into any trouble with the referee."

Eric won the PFA's Player of the Year award in 1994 and while his soccer exploits were overshadowed in '95 back at his modest three-bedroom semi in the Leeds suburb of Roundhay Eric's wife Isabelle stood by him.

Isabelle lectures in French at Leeds University and their six-year-old son Raphael is happily settled at school. "I can't believe they call Eric aggressive," says Isabelle. "He's a fantastic father and very good company."

Eric, a painter and philosopher as well as a poet, met Isabelle, 32, when she was a 20-year-old student of philosophy and language at university in Aix-en-Provence and he was a 17-year-old apprentice at a college for football skills. They have been married seven years and Eric sums up his success simply. "My attitude has always been the same," he says. "Anything is possible if you put your mind to it."

Ryan Giggs

If Ryan answered every fan letter he received he would never make the 3pm kick-off on a Saturday afternoon.

United's tricky winger receives more than 2,000 each week, most of them from girls, and he's enlisted the help of his grandad to help sort them out.

At 21 Ryan literally has the world at his feet – good looking, fit, virtually a millionaire and one of the most talented footballers of his generation. But there was a time last season when the critics seemed to want to write him off as soccer's latest flash in the pan.

"My form dipped," Ryan said. " By having a few niggling injuries and then playing games when I wasn't 100 per cent fit just added to it. I was getting injured for two weeks, then training for two days, then playing a game. I just wasn't sharp enough or fit enough. I had my longest spell out of the first team and it was terrible. It isn't much fun sitting on the treatment table watching the other players training."

Ryan's erratic form was one of the talking points of United's ill-fated European Cup campaign and he accepts his share of the blame. "It was so frustrating after getting off to such a good start against Gothenburg. Everybody feels they let down the supporters, especially in the games in Spain and Sweden."

Hard work, an understanding manager and full fitness soon saw the real Giggs return and he rates his best performance the 3-2 away victory over Chelsea.

"I didn't really do anything special, though I made the goal for Mark Hughes," explained Ryan. "But I think I gave the ball away only once. Not giving the ball away is something I've really tried to work on. Sometimes I can be sloppy in my passes but against Chelsea I thought my passing was spot on."

Ryan lives alone in North Manchester, though he still has a large circle of friends from his schooldays. He also often pops round to visit Paul Ince, his best mate at Old Trafford.

He split with girlfriend Dani Behr from TV's The Word early in '95, a break-up he blames on the Press. "With Dani the press was unbelievable," he says. "Now the press puts me off relationships. I've had cameramen camped outside the house just waiting to see if a girl stays overnight. It's stupid. Most of the other players are married or have long-term girlfriends so it doesn't affect them. Only a few of us are single. I'd like to get married one day and have kids though I don't know when yet." Ryan is the son of Welshman Danny Wilson, whose reputation for drinking and womanising eclipsed a top class rugby career with first Cardiff and then professionally with Rugby League club Swinton. Ryan was raised by his mother Lynn in Salford.

He can rely on home life to keep his feet on the ground. "My family and friends keep any superstar nonsense out of my head," says Ryan.

Ryan, 5ft 11ins and 11st 6lbs, captained the England schools football team, was the youngest-ever Welsh international at 17 and signed as a junior for United in 1990. He made his full debut, scoring the only goal in a match against Everton the following season. His favourite food is pasta and his favourite pastime buying clothes.

Andrei Kanchelskis

There have been few more exciting sights at Old Trafford than Andrei flying down the right wing, beating a couple of defenders and blasting another unstoppable shot past the opposing goalkeeper.

Unfortunately, such sweet memories turned a little sour in 1995 when Andrei asked for a transfer, disappointed at being left out of the team.

Andrei had been complaining of a mysterious stomach problem since before Christmas despite undergoing two negative scans.

The Ukranian believed United were refusing to take seriously his repeated claims that something was wrong.

However, on April 19 he underwent a stomach operation to repair a damaged muscle and fears of a serious hernia problem were dismissed. His relationship with Alex Ferguson, however, was undermined and there were serious doubts as to whether he would see through his five-year contract.

Thankfully on May 12 he agreed to stay on and Ferguson said: "There's been a lot of talk about Andrei being unsettled, but I think that was because of the problems we had diagnosing his injury and communication difficulties. It was really just a misunderstanding. With the operation successfully behind him and a better understanding we resolved the situation."

Despite Andrea's problems he remained one of United's top goalscorers in '94-'95 – the highlight being a magnificent hat-trick in the 5-0 derby victory over Manchester City at Old Trafford.

On top of that no United fan will ever forget the two goals he scored against Blackburn at Ewood Park in October. Andrei, whose dad is a lorry driver in Kivogra, joined United in May 1991 for £1 million from Shaktyor Donetsk. His dazzling runs and spectacular goals were a feature of United's Championship successes and all by a player who developed his speed and athleticism as an ice hockey player.

Andrei and his wife Inna live with their first child Andrei Andreevich in a mews house in Altrincham. He has more than 30 Russian caps.

Andrei, 26, does most of his talking through the lips of George Scanlan, the interpreter who United also employed to help Eric Cantona. Even after four years Andrei still speaks to Scanlan frequently and after every game Scanlan is first on the pitch to extend a handshake.

Brian McClair

If ever a player deserved a medal for loyalty it has to be Brian. He had found himself sitting on the bench for large parts of the 93-94 season. There was never a hint of complaint.

And last year he received his reward, performing a pivotal role in

Alex Ferguson's plans. He made 35 full appearances and another five as substitute in the Premiership and also starred in United's glittering FA Cup run.

He scored in the 5-2 fourth round victory over Wrexham and the fifth round 3-1 win against Leeds. He would probably have given up both those strikes, however, if only he could have conjured up one more to go with his equaliser in the last nail-biting game of the season at West Ham when victory would have given United the title.

Brian was Fergie's first major signing, costing United £850,000 from Celtic in 1987 and his manager is his biggest fan. "Brian is a great pro who does the business in whatever role he is given," says Fergie.

Brian could easily, however, have had a career outside football. He studied for a Bsc in maths for two years at Glasgow University while playing part-time football with Motherwell in 1981-82 and only gave up the course when Celtic offered him a four-year contract.

"A job as a maths teacher has always appealed to me," he says. He signed for Celtic in 1983 scoring 122 goals in four years. In his first season with United "Chocky," as he is known to his team-mates, was top scorer with 31 goals. Away from football Brian adores listening to music and is a rock and pop expert.

He also loves video games and playing with his home computer which he uses for teaching his three children, Siobhan, 7, Laura, 5, and Liam, 3, at his Cheshire home which he shares with wife Maureen.

David May

David travelled only 25 miles from Ewood Park to Old Trafford when he joined United but he realised at once he had crossed the great divide.

"I knew I was swapping one of the biggest clubs in England for one of the greatest in the world," said David, who severed a 10-year association at Blackburn for a £5,000-a-week pay packet at United.

"When we travelled to Ireland for a pre-season friendly we were literally besieged by fans," added David. "Some of them even camped outside the hotel just to get an autograph. And we were mobbed when we did a signing day in Manchester."

David, a policeman's son from Oldham, joined Blackburn at 13 after trials with his first love ironically Manchester City. The great mystery is that he was allowed to walk out of Ewood without a fight after being told his £3,000-a-week wage claims were excessive.

"All I ever wanted was a decent wage," says David. "But Blackburn's first offer was an insult. They seemed to look at me and think 'This is a lad who has been here since he was a kid. He'll sign eventually'."

Blackburn's loss was United's gain and David, who graduated from the same Boundary Park junior club which spawned David Platt and Mark Robins, started the season at right back. He scored his first goal for United in the 2-0 home win over Port Vale in the Coca Cola Cup in October.

And though he was in and out of the team for much of the season, plagued by various injuries and loss of form, he popped up in May to score one of United's most vital goals – a close range strike in the 1-0 home win against Sheffield Wednesday.

Nicky Butt

Former England captain Jimmy Armfield, who has watched successive generations of players develop and who is now officially responsible for part of that process, has little doubt about 20-year-old Butt's potential.

"It would not surprise me if Butt doesn't figure in the senior squad as soon as the European Championships next summer," said Armfield.

"I watched him play for the Under-21 side against the Irish and there is no doubt about his stature. He can tackle, he is comfortable on either foot and he gets into the penalty area. There isn't much missing from his game."Nicky is so natural on the ball he sometimes scares Fergie. There was one moment of supreme over-confidence when United were clinging to their 3-2 lead at Coventry late in the season which saw Fergie leaping from his dug-out to remonstrate with his teenage star.

"He was playing bloody one-twos on the edge of our penalty area," Fergie said with disbelief afterwards. "I suppose it shows the boy's composure, but at the time you have your heart in your mouth."

Paul Scholes

Alex Ferguson compared Paul's striking talents to those of Denis Law after his two goals against QPR in December gave United a vital 3-2 victory. That's a tough act to follow but seven goals in just 10 full appearances, with another dozen as sub, suggests a golden future.

Paul Parker

What a difference a year makes. In the Double winning season England international Paul was Alex Ferguson's Mr Reliable, playing in all their 42 League games. Last season he made just three full appearances in all competitions as the injury jinx, which has dogged him through his career, struck again.

Gary Walsh

Dependable goalkeeping understudy, Gary performed a crucial role when Peter Schmeichel was sidelined for two months with a back injury. Gary played in 10 Premiership games, conceding just 12 goals. He also played three times in the European Cup and three times in the Coca Cola Cup competition.

David Beckham

Scored in the European Cup against Galatasaray and made seven full appearances. Another of Fergie's fledglings he spent part of the season gaining experience on loan to Preston where he scored on his debut.

Simon Davies

No doubt what was the highlight of 21-year-old winger Simon's eight full first team appearances – his goal in the 4-0 home victory over Galatasaray in the European Cup.

Chris Casper

Promising young fullback who at 20 made his only appearance of the season in the 2-0 home victory over Port Vale in the Coca Cola Cup second round second leg.

Keith Gillespie

Made six first team appearances before being transferred to Newcastle as part of the 7m deal which brought Andy Cole to Old Trafford.

Phil Neville

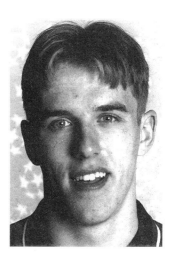

Like his big brother, United defender Gary Neville, nineteen-year-old Phil is a tall, athletic defender who made two appearances in the 94-95 season one in the Premiership against Manchester City and in the FA Cup fourth round against Wrexham.

John O'Kane

Twenty-year-old fullback who played two games, one as substitute and one full appearance in the 2-0 FA Cup victory at Sheffield United.

Alex Ferguson

When Old Trafford chairman Martin Edwards praised Alex Ferguson from Aberdeen in 1986 he was convinced he had hired a manager capable of shaping United's destiny into the next century.

There can be no doubt that he appointed the right man. Yes, he has brought phenomenal success over the last five years but the way Fergie handled the disappointment of losing the Premiership crown in such dramatic circumstances at Upton Park told much about his strength of character and dignified leadership.

There were no excuses from the man whose job was made so difficult by problems involving Cantona, and Keane, as well as disruptive injuries to Giggs, Kanchelskis, Hughes, Parker and May.

He swallowed the disappointment of the 1-1 draw with West Ham to tell Blackburn boss Kenny Dalglish: "You deserve it. All credit to Blackburn. Anyone who gets 89 points deserves the Championship. Most Leagues are won in the mid-80s. Blackburn have gone well beyond that which is because of us. It's taken a very good team to take our Championship and we could not have done more to stop them than we did at West Ham.

"It was a marvellous, fantastic performance by my players – you get your money's worth watching us. I'm proud of them all. Over the last four years we've contested four Championships and lost only 22 games out of 168. That's magnificent and they can be proud of themselves."

Everyone at Old Trafford is equally proud of Ferguson, born in Govan, Glasgow on New Year's Eve,1941, and the son of a Clyde shipyard worker. His enthusiasm and appetite for work is legendary at Old Trafford. As a player he made his debut for Queen's Park in 1957 and had spells with St Johnstone and Dunfermline. He signed for Rangers in 1967 and also played for Falkirk and Ayr.

His first management post was with East Stirling. From there he joined Aberdeen where he collected a string of major honours including the European Cup Winners' Cup.

Alex is married with three grown-up children and has received the OBE for services to soccer. He took over the Scotland manager's job on a temporary basis following Jock Stein's death in 1986 but turned down the permanent post.

Under Ferguson United have won the FA Cup (1990 and 94), the European Cup Winners' Cup (1991), the European Super Cup (1991), the Football League Cup (1992), and the Premiership trophy (1993 and 1994).

The Future

When the dust settled on the season Alex Ferguson was already planning his Last Hurrah. The Manchester United manager will give himself at least two more years in charge of England's most celebrated club before moving upstairs as a director.

His immediate aim is to claw back the championship from Blackburn for another tilt at the European Cup. He covets that prize above all others. The last two seasons of failure in the arena of champions has merely increased Ferguson's yearning. At 53 the fires still burn as fiercely in his psyche as they did when he started trophy collecting at Aberdeen 17 years ago.

It will do him no harm to look 26 miles up the road at Kenny Dalglish's new Ewood empire knowing he is no longer the irresistible force of the nineties.

Alex Ferguson remains the workaholic of Old Trafford, the first professional on duty at the club daily. He rarely arrives at his training ground office later than 7.45 a.m. The challenge remains daunting, maybe unique. Blackburn, bankrolled by owner Jack Walker to the tune of £60 million with more promised, have the financial clout to make themselves the new Colossus of English club football. Even United with their vast gates and gargantuan commercial operation are stretched to joust in the financial arena with Ewood's Uncle Jack.

Ferguson's other challenge is how best to mix and match his young players - the sweetest crop since the Busby Babes - with the aspirations of the club and fans. When the United manager invested in Andy Cole he gave himself a problem that would have ushered Mark Hughes out but for Eric Cantona's brainstorm at Selhurst Park a fortnight later. It could easily have destroyed attacker Paul Scholes. Scholes, tenacious young midfielder Nicky Butt, brothers Gary and Philip Neville and the creative David Beckham are United's future just as much as Ryan Giggs.

Twice last season the entire United kindergarten was called up as a unit and responded by beating First Division Port Vale away and at home in the Coca Cola Cup.

Ferguson made it clear, that when the best talent becomes available he will try to hire it. Especially if the player happens to be English.

"I have always considered the player you produce is better than the one you buy" says Ferguson. But the cheque book remains ready.

Cole's arrival on January 10 took Ferguson's spending past

Blackburn's Dalglish to more than 30 million on 27 players in little over eight years.

But when he does quit his desk to join the crowd upstairs, Fergie will hand to his successor a dressing room young enough to take United into the next millenium.

That, as much as the success of great imported stars like Cantona, Cole, Ince, Kanchelskis and Schmeichel, will give him cause for private congratulation.

Who will follow Fergie? The United job, above all others, is a time bomb. After Busby, five managers were broken by its demands, until Ferguson finally gave the club the stature of champions after 26 years.

He has a unique insight into the crushing pressure of Old Trafford. And Ferguson has made it clear that when the time comes he would be happy to hand over to his assistant Brian Kidd. "If he wants it the job is his" he says.

But a faction in the Boardroom would undoubtedly like to bring back Bryan Robson after his instant promotion success with Middlesbrough.

The immediate future? Cantona remains the player to get the championship momentum going again. The Frenchman is still the most gifted individual in the British game, able to turn and win a match with a spasm of brilliance. Next season he will link up front with Cole - the liaison Fergie had in mind when he hired the young Newcastle star. It puffs up another cloud of doubt above the dark head of Mark Hughes. The Frenchman's return in September could push Hughes towards the exit door again.

Or will it? The million dollar question remains: Can Ferguson control Cantona's notorious temperament, especially on opposition grounds where the fans are ganging up to bait him?

Without him their effectiveness is visibly impaired. His four-month absence almost certainly cost them last season's title. Yet such is the quality and charisma of the man his decision to reject Inter Milan and sign a new three-year deal for United was greeted by a communal gasp of relief by everyone at Old Trafford - not the least the manager.

Cantona could yet turn out to be the saint of Fergie's Last Hurrah.

Acknowledgements

With grateful thanks to Bill Chalmers at
HarperCollinsManufacturing
Ron Taylor at Keene Repro

Colin Eyre at The Imaging Business,
Jeremy Alexander and Tom Gorham
for all their help and expertise

The Great Matches by John Bean
Pen Pictures by Frank Malley
The Future by John Bean

Thanks to Daily Express Chief Soccer Writer Steve Curry.
Northern Soccer Correspondent, John Bean and other members
of the Express team: John Wragg, Jim Holden, Kevin Moseley,
Richard Lewis, Matt Dickinson, John Keith
and John Donoghue

Also to Frances Jennings for sorting out
the system and providing the disks and
to Matthew Emery for picture research.

All pictures used are from the library of
Express Newspapers plc